In Therapy

T0161509

SUSIE ORBACH is a psychotherapist, psychoanalyst, writer and social critic. She is a co-founder of the Women's Therapy Centre of London, a former *Guardian* columnist and visiting professor at the London School of Economics and the author of a number of books, including *What Do Women Want?* (with Luise Eichenbaum), *On Eating, Hunger Strike, The Impossibility of Sex, Bodies* – which won the Women in Psychology Prize – and the international bestseller *Fat is a Feminist Issue*, which has sold well over a million copies and been continuously in print in the UK. *The New York Times* said, 'She is probably the most famous psychotherapist to have set up couch in Britain since Sigmund Freud.' She lives in London and lectures extensively worldwide.

Also by Susie Orbach

Bodies

On Eating

The Impossibility of Sex

Towards Emotional Literacy

What's Really Going on Here

Hunger Strike

Fat is a Feminist Issue

Fat is a Feminist Issue II

By Susie Orbach and Luise Eichenbaum

Bittersweet: Love, Competition & Envy in Women's Relationships

What Do Women Want? Exploding the Myth of Dependency

Understanding Women: A Feminist Psychanalytic Approach

Outside In Inside Out: A Feminist and Psychoanalytical Approach to Women's Psychology

Edited by Susie Orbach, Lisa Appignanesi and Rachel Holmes

Fifty Shades of Feminism

In Therapy

The Unfolding Story

Susie Orbach

PROFILE BOOKS

This revised and extended edition published in 2018
First published in Great Britain in 2016 by
PROFILE BOOKS LTD
3 Holford Yard
Bevin Way
London WC1X 9HD
www.profilebooks.com

Published in association with Wellcome Collection

183 Euston Road
London NW1 2BE
www.wellcomecollection.org

By arrangement with the BBC
The BBC Radio 4 logo is a trade mark of the British Broadcasting
Corporation and is used under licence.

5 7 9 10 8 6

Typeset in Photina by MacGuru Ltd

Printed and bound by CPI Group (UK) Ltd, Croydon, CR0 4YY

A CIP catalogue record for this book is available from the British Library.

ISBN 978 1 78125 988 7
eISBN 978 1 78283 431 1

Contents

For Jeanette Winterson, again. My quest to share
what goes on in the consulting room.

Introduction: Turning a Full Stop into a Comma

People come to therapy when avenues for understanding themselves or moving forward stall. They come because love has gone wrong, because they are frozen in unsatisfactory work or intimate relationships, because they have lost touch with themselves, because they are searching for authenticity, because they don't know how to let go, because their life is falling in on them, because they have suffered events so bruising they don't know how to assimilate them.

They come in pain, in confusion, sometimes in sorrow, sometimes bewildered or frightened by their behaviour, sometimes in anger, sometimes to express grievances. They can be full of words and yet devoid of the ones they need to express the underlying confusions. They can be full of emotions which repeat on them because the emotion that engulfs them is part of the problem covering over more subtle feelings which don't have a home in the person's sense of self. They can be full of ideas, of theories about why misfortune has befallen them.

The work of therapy is to open up these three levels: feelings, words and ideas. It aims to crack open the existing words, the existing emotions and the existing ideas. Therapy tries to slow the person (or the couple or group) sufficiently to hear, feel and think what they are saying and to have it heard by the therapist.

Words, and how they are said, take on special significance. There may be few of them, with gaps and hesitations in between. They can come tumbling out, and yet what they are saying may misfire, too jumbled to yield their truths immediately. Therapy takes the time to listen closely. To find entry points so that contradictory thoughts and feelings can surface and be acknowledged, so angers can be heard, disappointments felt, anxieties unpicked. In that hearing, a person or a couple can know themselves, their motivations, their feelings, their understandings of self, more deeply.

Therapy doesn't seek to *fix* the problem in a simplistic way, although good therapy always addresses the problem that is brought in. Therapy's aim is to understand, to provide context, to indicate ways of thinking, feeling and being that invite the individual to know more of her- or himself, to extend their experience, to intervene in stumbling blocks or hurtful practices, to live more richly. Conflicts may remain but are often transformed. There are always reiterations but now ideas about the source of pain shift about. Where there may have been one word or one emotion to explain oneself to oneself, there may be several words and feelings and even ideas that sit alongside one another. A clamp one didn't know existed is released.

Where there once was a full stop, there can now be a comma. And where there was only a past or a future, there can be a present, informed by an examined past which can welcome rather than fear a future.

The consulting room is a place of reflection, of intense and yet often quiet conversing, thinking and feeling. The stories here encompass loss, shame, intergenerational conflict, the impact of illness, parenting, challenges of late life, life's disappointments, the role of faith, belonging, love, hurt, achieving, connecting, failing, mothers and daughters, fathers and sons, longing, wanting and transitions. Examining these themes as we read along beckons us and the analysands to find ourselves, anew.

Susie Orbach, *December 2017*

Douglas

First Session

Douglas rang me, breathless. He had asked around about who he should see as he was in an emergency, and he found his way to my consulting room. He is sixty-four and portly, a grammar-school boy who grew up in the Midlands.

Douglas   Hello, Susie.

Susie   Hello.

Douglas   I'm Douglas. Sorry I am late, traffic was terrible and it's quite a way. So I am a bit pressured timewise.

He claps to indicate that we should get started.

Susie   So, tell me.

Douglas   Well, I mean, I don't know how this process works, I really don't.

I have never done this before. As you know from my email, I heard about you from a friend and I thought I would try this route because I am having some problems really, and I wanted to see if you could offer me anything or help me with this problem.

It is a problem really with anger, which is affecting me in my work, in my life and, well I need some advice really, some help, because I am worried that I am going to damage myself professionally. Really that's the issue I am worried about, the way I am in my job, and I need … I need some help with this anger issue. I am angry all the time, I am angry in my work, I am angry with the world and I really need to know what I do with the issues that flood into my brain.

Susie	Are you angry right now?
Douglas	Ah, well, I'm – yes, I am rather, yes, because I don't know how this works, I don't know what to say, I don't know how to proceed.
Susie	Can I just slow you?
Douglas	Yeah, sure, sorry.
Susie	I am intrigued that you said you are angry now because you don't know how it works.
Douglas	Yeah.
Susie	Could you bear to not know how it works?
Douglas	I mean this is all new to me, I have never really talked about this before to anybody, let alone a therapy person, so I am rather nervous actually.
Susie	So you are nervous right now?

Douglas says he's angry because he doesn't know how this works. I find this useful in getting a sense of how wide the scope of his anger is. To the 'logical' mind not knowing doesn't necessarily engender anger, so Douglas helpfully gives me another dimension to his anger.

Susie	Well, I would like to help you, I would like to hear a little bit more about you.
Douglas	About me.
Susie	Uh-huh.
Douglas	Well, I am sixty-four. My name is Douglas Stapley. I am a judge. I am currently sitting on a case at Southwark Crown Court, and really that's the issue that has brought me here, because it is beginning to affect the way I do my work and it is worrying me.

Susie   What is the case?

Douglas   It is a case of a chap accused of GBH [*Grievous Bodily Harm*]
              and sex trafficking. He is involved in a criminal gang that
              imports girls, usually from Eastern Europe, and puts them
              in massage parlours, some in London, some in Leeds,
              and he has been arrested for GBH against one of these
              women. He is a very nasty man and he is – well, I can't
              really say more about the case but I am worried about my
              reaction to him.

Susie   What is your reaction?

Douglas   I want to kill him. Of course, I shouldn't say that, but um …

Susie   Well, it's privileged in here.

Therapists and clients have privileged status unless there is a real
danger, in which case reporting may be required. If we learn of
an intent to commit a serious criminal offence, to harm oneself or
others, we may break confidentiality. See, for example, www.bpc.
org.uk, 'Statement on Confidentiality'.

Douglas   Yes, good. Um, I am furious with him, I am furious with his
              counsel, I am furious with what he represents, the people
              who stand behind him who will never be arrested or
              extradited. I am furious with the way the world is going,
              and I just don't know what to do with this angst and this
              anger about things I see on the news and things I see in
              my courtroom.

              It is beginning to overwhelm me, and of course I am
              meant to be objective.

              I am meant to dispense justice in a calm and rational way,
              and I am feeling I am losing my ability to do that.

He comes to a full stop. He looks like he has drifted off somewhere.

Susie   Please go on.

Douglas   Sorry, I beg your pardon.

He pauses again and starts speaking slowly.

Douglas   Something happened to me last week in the course of this
               trial that had never happened before. I had to call a recess
               that went on for more than an hour while I tried to recover
               myself in my chambers and in the gentlemen's toilet, and I
               couldn't conduct the trial because it was just beginning to
               overwhelm me, my rage, and I am worried I am going to
               lose my judgeship actually.

Susie   Do you know what – can you remember what exactly
               happened before you called the recess?

Douglas   Yes.

Susie   What was going on in the trial?

Douglas   This man's counsel has called what I laughingly call a
               character witness, and he was cross-examining him on the
               stand. I found the machinations of the defence counsel
               completely intolerable, the excuses, the mitigations, the
               excuses for this low-level, violent bully and this character
               witness who, as it turned out, hadn't actually met or
               seen the man whose character he was testifying for, for
               a matter of twelve, thirteen, fourteen years, um, and
               I stopped the – I actually lost my temper in court and
               shouted at the defence counsel. I abused the witness
               verbally and I, as it were, saw a red mist descending and
               I just had to leave, because the thing is, this defence
               counsel, he is a very clever, very sly man. He knows me

from other cases and he will, if he can, call for a retrial if I lose myself in that way again, and I am fearful that I will. He has told his client that he might get away with a suspended sentence.

Well, he is going to find that he might end up with a life sentence and I am just worried that if it is appealed, which it will be, I might …

Susie Because of your anger.

Douglas Because of my anger and because of certain other instances in the courtroom where the defence counsel could make a case that the judge is unbalanced.

Susie Douglas, could you tell me what the defence's argument is briefly?

Douglas About his client?

Susie Yes, about their client.

Douglas He is saying that he is not really violent, that the instance of violence for which he is on trial was an aberration, that he had a difficult upbringing, that he is a family man with children who would be deprived of their father if he was in prison, that he actually – and this is the one that really got to me – he actually put him forward as caring for the girls that he is trafficking and being a protector father figure if you will. And I mean, the thing is, I really want to kill this man.

Susie So beyond the ethics or the politics, which I can empathise with, is there anything else that might be leading you to want to kill him? Is there something in his story that resonates at another level?

This is an open question. It could be he has a niece who is shielding a trafficked young woman, or a brother who married a Thai bride. Therapists are often thought to have X-ray eyes. We don't. We have questions that can turn a mirror on the self.

Douglas   Um … yes … he reminds me of something in myself, I think. Um, it is as though his violence and his, in a way, his rage, which came out in this attack on this woman, it just mirrors my own, and I think that disturbs me.

Um, he … I think he, um …

There is a type of man that I hate and I always have hated, I find myself not listening to the evidence but looking at him in the dock and having fantasies of violence against him as though I know him personally, as though he has personally hurt me.

Susie   Uh-huh. Well, he has hurt you personally in the sense that you experience his behaviour as an affront, but I think you are saying something else about that.

Douglas   I have a friend who is a vicar, who I mentioned this to in passing, and I am not really a believer, but I was so desperate I would do anything, talk to anybody, and he said look at Luke, Chapter 6, which I did, and I had heard of the words before, of course – 'judge not that ye be not judged', and 'do unto others as you would have them do unto you' – it is all that stuff which is meant to be the credo by which I practise my profession and I find that I can't do that any more. I can't do it in the face of what is happening in the world.

I suppose what I want to ask you is what do I *do* with all this rage and angst in my courtroom against this man, but also against leaders of the world and violent people in the world who create wars, who create suffering? It is beginning to overwhelm me and I fear, not exactly for my sanity, but I certainly fear for my ability to do my job because how can I judge him when I feel guilty too, as it were?

Even in the few moments of our speaking together, Douglas has become very thoughtful. He's afraid, yes, but he is also questioning how to handle himself, how to make sense of the emotional discomfort he's beset by. I'm a small woman, but I almost feel my physicality expand to meet him so that his confusions will have enough space inside of me too without belittling him.

Susie   We are talking about two different kinds of GBH. We are talking about what you feel about what is going on in the world and what he has done in the world, and I am wondering what you think *you* have done in the world, or what you have done in your private world that disturbs you that is violent or doesn't fit with your ethics.

Does that make any sense?

Douglas   Yes. I wonder. Sorry, my driver is outside and I need to go.

Susie   That's fine, but I need to know in order to be able to be of any use to you Douglas.

Douglas   Umm. Well I suppose we all have secrets, and mine is, as it were, surfacing in this trial because this man, much as I despise him, is only providing a market, if you will, for men who wish to buy sexual favours from these girls, and that is something that I have done, yes.

Susie   And for that you hate yourself?

Douglas   I hate my anger at this man.

Susie   Yeah, I know, but could we just parse it a little better, or a little more fully?

Douglas   What does that word mean, parse?

Susie   Well, you know, we did it in grammar in school, break down what you are actually saying, into its parts of speech.

Douglas   Break down. Um.

Susie   You said you hate yourself for having taken …

Douglas   I hate myself for having given this man a reason to do what he does, and so how can I judge him?

[*Clap. Long pause.*]

I have to judge him because I am a judge.

Susie   So as you are telling me this, I am sensing there is another feeling coming across that isn't quite anger. A sense of shame and hurt. Does that mean anything to you?

Douglas   Yes, I am deeply ashamed.

Susie   You are ashamed of the act and you are ashamed of yourself, and so you can't find any compassion towards yourself. Would that be right?

Douglas   I am ashamed of the act, yes. I am ashamed of the hypocrisy that I find myself demonstrating. I am ashamed of – I am very – I find sexual matters very shaming and, um, this case coming before me has brought that to the surface, I think, so I feel ashamed and I find that my shame is becoming anger at him and I am losing the ability to distinguish between the two emotions in the court.

In a way I should acquit him, [*clap*] I should give him a suspended sentence.

There is no time for me to unpick with Douglas the shame he experiences towards sexual matters. His shame is driving his aggression as though to keep the whole thing as far away from him as possible. At the same time his identification inclines him to put himself in the same category as the trafficker. His thinking is glued up because we are just beginning to explore these difficult issues.

Susie   How much longer is the case going on for?

Douglas   About another week. The jury will retire at the beginning of next week, and then I expect – he will be found guilty, [*clap*] and then I have to sum up to the jury of course before that, and then I have to pass sentence, which will be two days later, after the end of the trial.

Susie   Well, can I suggest this, can I suggest that we meet again, very soon?

Douglas   Yes.

Susie   Before your summing up?

Douglas   Yes.

Susie   I think it is important that you have been able to make the link and if we can loosen it a little bit, you might feel safer in the courtroom. So if you could come next Monday.

Douglas   Yes.

Susie   Before court.

Douglas   Early.

Susie   Yes, come at 8.30.

Douglas   I know you are a feminist. I have looked at your book titles, although I haven't had time to read them, and I, I, I am ashamed as well. I hope you won't be angry with me in the way that I am angry with him.

Susie   See you next week.

Douglas, understandably, is seeking reassurance that I won't judge him. Perhaps the reader is wondering why I couldn't have responded with a soothing word. I felt that this latter remark about my being a feminist was diverting us into the issue of judgement and taking away from what Douglas had been able to talk about just before. I had no wish to add to his discomfort, but I felt that I would be softening the links he had just made for himself. I had offered another session right after that weekend and hoped that would be sufficiently containing. As for the issue of judgement, him as the judge, me as the judge, these fascinating questions are in my mind and I anticipate will be part of what we talk about in the future.

Douglas is coming in an emergency. It is often like this. There is no space for history. Only the immediate present. Urgency is what drives him, and the question is how the therapist responds to that emergency while knowing that emergencies come and go.

I know I can't provide a solution. I can hope, however, even in his first session, to slow things down enough to make some pockets of air in his head so he is less overwhelmed by rage and the fear that he will act inappropriately. Obviously in therapy we don't do this by suggesting the individual could take a specific course of action as a colleague might. We do it by trying to expand his thinking, his feelings and his stance towards his dilemma.

I also want to slow him down enough so that I have a way of entering into his world: how his mind, his thinking, his body, his feelings work. If a therapist is to work in any sustained way with someone, then they have to get as close to the experience of the person as possible. They have to 'walk in their shoes' sufficiently to understand. But we have to do this while thinking through the manner in which the individual makes the links they do which lead them to full stops.

Second Session

Douglas   Hello.

Susie   Hello Douglas.

Douglas   Nice to see you again.

Susie   You too.

Douglas   Thank you. So, thank you for the last – thank you.

I, um, I shall have to be in court in an hour and a half, and I have to sum up and I have to, really, I have to decide what I am going to do with this man who I find so challenging. So I am in a quandary really because I want to punish him severely and I suppose I feel that I should be punished too, and if I am lenient with him it is an injustice because the man is an appalling criminal. If I am hard with him, I am a complete hypocrite because he is only doing something that I have helped to create.

Susie   Could you tell me a little bit more about your relationship to the women you see him trafficking?

Douglas   My relationship with them.

Susie   Well, to women who you have bought sex from.

Douglas   Oh God. You see, I think I never quite understood why certain things that the world thinks are wrong are wrong. When I was younger, I was guilt-free really about using women in that way, and …

Well, that's not quite true.

The magic of therapy is that it allows space for the person to go back on themselves and question their actions and their motivation. Therapy is not a linear process where a line of enquiry is followed sequentially. It is about associations made, the stuck places, the hot spots, the confusion which we come at in different ways, and while a therapist may ask a question, it isn't the answer per se that is important but what it can open up for the individual.

Susie   Uh-huh.

Douglas   My relationship with these girls is quite perfunctory, of course, because you don't get to know them, but I did have romantic fantasies about a certain girl especially but – and I think in a way that allowed me to feel guilt-free because I thought, well, I am treating them as human, I am not violent, I pay them very well, I asked one of them to meet me outside, you know, which she refused – but I kind of feel that I was humane in my relationship with these girls, but there was one Polish girl who I got to know a bit, and who I realised was indeed trafficked, exploited and wanted me to help her. In fact, she was the last girl that I saw in this way.

Susie   How recent was this?

Douglas   This was a long time ago, ten years ago. Um, and I feel guilty about her because I didn't quite realise at the time, but quite soon after I realised that she was frightened and in trouble, and needing to be liberated from the grip of a man like the man who is standing in the dock in front of me at this trial.

And I let her down because I did nothing.

I think I was ashamed and embarrassed about the possibility of being discovered. And so I walked away from that part of my life and buried it and left it, and I think it is these girls that I hear about now, this past week, have reignited this dilemma within me. I think I wanted love but I was paying for sex, and I kind of made that alright in my mind, and suddenly the anger has come up again with regard to this man and it is not alright.

Susie   Because not only does he exploit these women, but he exploits both their need for love and men's need for love?

Douglas   Yes, exactly, and that is why I said about your being a feminist, or women I have talked to about these things, without of course telling them of my own particular involvement. But I find sometimes that certain people, they don't see the man as a victim as well as the women.

Susie   Well, I wonder if you could see yourself as a victim.

Douglas   Yes I do, but then how can I be a victim?

Susie   Could you slow down a second, instead of rejecting it? This is a new idea for you, Douglas, and would you just consider it for more than a millisecond?

Douglas   Well, I have agreed with you. I mean I have agreed, I have agreed. You are right.

Douglas's voice turns irate. His whole body looks inflamed. Some of his vulnerability has shown itself and made him uneasy. I'm still on the mission helping him see how anger becomes a portmanteau emotion, carrying many different feelings.

Susie   I think this is really helpful because you are showing me a piece of where the anger comes from.

Douglas   I feel that you are going to judge me and punish me.

Susie   I am actually more interested in trying to understand and …

Douglas   I think you are like – it wasn't an accident that I came to you.

Susie   What, you came for punishment from a feminist? And you
                 are paying me very well.

Douglas   You're – I sit up there on the bench and I am very
                 powerful. Um, and I am very aware of my power and I feel
                 like a lonely child all at the same time.

Susie   And a lonely man?

Douglas   Yes, but I sit up there and I feel like a preposterous
                 ten-year-old wearing a wig. Actually not ten, more like
                 sixteen, um, with impossible – how can I do this job, how
                 can I judge people's emotions, behaviour, when I am so
                 confused, and I think … I knew you were of a certain type,
                 you are a woman, and I think I, ah, I, ah, yes, I don't know.

Susie   Do you think you really came here to be beaten up?

Douglas   I expected …

Susie   Unless you think that is a form of help.

Douglas   No, it is not a form of help.

Susie   Right. So I think you …

Douglas   But I mean what I did was bad, and what I am doing now
                 is bad and …

Susie   Well, I am interested in that, and I hope we will come to
                 understand it, but at the moment I have got this very
                 strong image, the one you just gave me, or gave us, of the
                 young man sitting up there in fancy dress.

Douglas   Um.

Susie   As though there can't be a vulnerable part of you at this
                 age, as though you have to somehow diminish your
                 vulnerability and speak of yourself as a sixteen-year-old
                 rather than you as a grown man, with a big job, who feels
                 vulnerable himself, and has complicated feelings.

Douglas   I think the difference is that this counsel who is arguing for this man – well, I know things about him, he has a complicated emotional life – but when I hear him, when I see him, he gets under my skin. It is as though I am looking at an adult with issues, with complications, and he makes me feel like a child, and that is the difference really. It is not like being an adult with vulnerability. I feel like a child sitting there, and I feel – the rage I feel, the tearfulness I feel when I had to call the recess, it was like being a child afflicted by a storm of emotion that I had no control over or context or perspective.

Susie   But actually it was very wise for you to call the recess, wasn't it?

Douglas   Well, I mean, it wasn't …

Susie   You were trying to take care of the situation, trying to take care of …

Douglas   I wasn't wise, it wasn't wise. It was just, if I hadn't done it I would have been sobbing in court.

Susie   Well, I guess that wouldn't have gone over big, so the fact that you knew …

Douglas   Well, it would have.

Susie   The fact that you knew that you might have been sobbing actually helps us a lot because sobbing is quite different from rage.

Douglas   Yes, they go together.

Susie   Well, do they?

Douglas   Rage leads to sadness, leads to rage, yes, they live together, one is the reverse of the other, two sides of the same coin.

Susie	Well, I'm intrigued by that because one bit doesn't seem to get much expression. What you have told me so far is that rage is the thing that gets expression. The sob is hidden.
Douglas	Well, I can't sob in court.
Susie	No, I accept that, but I think you are sobbing inside somewhere, and that is almost hidden from you and that is causing you difficulties.
Douglas	Um.
Susie	So that's worse than the rage, I don't mean in the public forum, I mean inside of you.
Douglas	Yes.

Now I feel we have done some parsing. We have been able to take apart what is bundled up by Douglas's response of rage. We have been able to identify his shame about his past behaviour, his disgust at the trafficker, his feelings of illegitimacy to judge another and his sobs about his predicament. I didn't pick up on what he knew of the defence counsel's 'complicated emotional life' because it would have broken the flow of dealing with the recognition of his own vulnerability, and that was primary. I was interested in what he was seeing or projecting on to the defence counsel that he thought he got away with while Douglas was beset with upset, anger and confusion. I set that aside in favour of exploring the feelings that came up that constitute his anger.

In my first session Douglas was angry because he didn't know how therapy worked, so now we have some of the elements of the bundle called rage which was scaring him. It is like a pressure sitting on top of a mix of contradictory feelings.

| Susie | You hurt in a lot of different ways. You are confused, and |

the rage is a kind of cover story for you endeavouring to hold yourself together, except it has got cracks in it.

Douglas Um, yes … I, um, yes.

Susie We have got to stop shortly, but one of the things that I am thinking about that must make this summing up so very difficult for you is that you want to convey empathy for the girls, the women, but you have kind of empathy deficit in relation to yourself, so you come in with the rage, and that is part of your dilemma.

Douglas Yes, because I want to punish him as well, I want to punish him very severely, so …

Susie But is there an interesting way of talking about the women's lives that would help you in this?

Douglas In what way?

Susie Well I'm not that au fait with summing up frankly, but I am thinking about not just the legal kernel here, but the fact of these women who you feel very affected by, who you feel have been so exploited, and wondering is there a way of you thinking about them in the summing up.

Douglas Yes.

Susie That might allow you some more space so that the rage doesn't overwhelm you.

Douglas Yes, I think, yes, I think I have this. I dreamt about it the other day. In fact I was in court and somebody at the back stood up and said I know what you've done, and how can I sentence the man, how can I sentence the man. I am sentencing him for violence but I am really sentencing him for casual cruelty and lack of empathy, that's the word you said.

Susie	Yes, but he is there because of GBH, because of the trafficking, the actual rounding up of women and the transporting of them.
Douglas	Yes, but they …
Susie	And the vulnerability of the women and the vulnerability they experience that you are trying to address.
Douglas	Um.
Susie	And privately the vulnerability of you, and other men who seek them.
	Look, we are going to have to stop now. I would like to see you on Thursday, and then if we wish to carry on after this emergency, we can discuss arrangements.
Douglas	Yes, that would be good, thank you.
Susie	OK.
Douglas	I shall think of you when I am in court. Thank you.

The sessions feel rushed on reading them, but in the room we had established a rapport which opened up some thinking and feeling space which levered Douglas out of his isolation and fear. I was moved by his ability to consider what was coming up in the sessions and I had every hope that he would be able to join up the sixteen-year-old in fancy dress with the substantial middle-aged man he is. Developing some compassion for his own difficulties and naming them were important in the very short term. As our sessions progressed, I sensed that the themes we talked of would be what we would look at in-depth, as we reflected on his history and the way it had closed down certain emotions for him.

I am aware that the practice of adversarial law is one kind of enquiry and that psychoanalytic therapy is another. In one, to put it crudely, we are looking to judge right and wrong. The crime has to be punished. In therapy, we hear multiple truths with different weights to them. The constraints of his summing up have legal ramifications, and not surprisingly Douglas expects to be judged in the therapy room both because of his work and because he is not accustomed to the modes of thinking in the consulting room which are about understanding not judgement per se.

Amelia and Grace

First Session (Amelia)

Amelia is in her early forties. She came in to talk about recent concerns about her daughter. She is middle-class, a stay-at-home mother with bits of work. Her husband, Grace's father, is travelling and rarely around. She speaks in a breathy manner and at speed. There is enormous tension in her hands, which she cups from one to the other.

Susie	Hello.
Amelia	Hello, it is Amelia here.
Susie	Come on all the way up to the top and I will meet you there.
Amelia	Right, thank you.
Susie	Come in.
Amelia	Hi, thank you.
Susie	I'm Susie.
Amelia	Hello, I'm Amelia.
Susie	Please take a seat on the sofa.
Amelia	Thank you, right. Lovely smells.
Susie	Umm.
Amelia	Right, well, can I take my jacket off?
Susie	Please do. I can hang it.
Amelia	I have been thinking about seeking some help or advice or something for a while, because I am having problems with my daughter Grace, but you know, listening to other mothers and other parents at the school, you know it just

seems to be sort of normal, but then I kind of think that her behaviour isn't normal and I am worried about her, but then I suddenly realise that I was worried about me, I think, and then, you know, I can't actually cope with her. And I think, I think … well we have had a massive row and I just, I don't know what to do.

Susie   So, do you want to tell me about the row or do you want to tell me about the behaviour that's disturbing you, or your behaviour in the situation?

This is instrumental, to invite Amelia to dissect what she has shared, and it is also simply a bridge to say I'm listening and please go on. This is Amelia's first experience of therapy, and on a technical level I want to introduce her to the ways of exploring we do in therapy while respecting, of course, her idiom. It is always difficult disrupting conventional ways of talking.

Amelia   Well, we've always been – when she was younger, she was very close to her dad, but in recent years he is sort of not around as much, and so, and we have become very, we had become very close, and now I don't know … it's like she woke up one day and was somebody else, and it is kind of impossible, it is impossible to know how to negotiate my way around her, and I can't, I just don't feel close to her any more and I just don't know what to do about that.

Susie   She woke up one day and she was rejecting, she was surly, she was what?

Amelia   She's, you know, her room started to sort of deteriorate into this kind of bomb site so you can't see the floor when you walk in the room, and you try and do everything to encourage her to tidy that, which ends up in a row every time, and you know she has also become quite dirty, so instead of, instead of washing something or putting it in the washing machine or in the bin to be washed, she will turn it inside out and put it back on again and that's just not acceptable, and so, you know, and you know, so I worry about all of that, and then there is just this astonishing relationship with her phone, there is – you know that it just sort of feels like it is an addiction and it is worrying me a lot because I feel as if it's – you know she is very, very talented, she is doing a lot of GCSEs, she is very clever, she is very popular, she is very liked by her teacher, she has absolutely no direction at all, which drives me insane, and to be so clever and not to focus it in any way, I just think is kind of really wrong.

I find that, I find that disturbing. What has triggered this is a row over the phone because I said she couldn't have it in her room after a certain time and she decided she needed it for her apps for her homework and stuff, and so … and her music, because she listens to pounding music while she is revising. I mean, I don't know how any child can do that, I don't know how anybody could do that, but she does, and so it is just, I just, I don't feel as if I can get anywhere near her to …

Susie   You said something, that when you talk to the other parents, the other mums, they are all having this experience.

Amelia   To a certain degree, yes, yes they are, yep. Um, I think, you know, I think, I think Grace, it just … I think it is difficult because she is very bright and very popular, it is not good for her within the social environment in the school I don't think, you know, I think she is going to start causing problems.

Susie   What kind of problems are you worried about?

I have registered what you said, that she has become dirty, that her room is a bomb site and that she lives on her phone, which I think is pretty typical for that age group.

Amelia   Right, right.

Susie   Not that that is easy for you to cope with and it is quite hard to set boundaries such as we are eating now, you don't use your phone, or whatever you work out. But I am not sure I have quite the measure of what you are so worried about.

Amelia   [*Laughing*] That is a very good question. I am probably worried about, I am probably really worried about losing her, because you know we are, we are very, very close and um, you know she is very rude now, very offensively rude. The other day she said – I was on my laptop – she said that my hands look veiny and that really upset me, and then I went to give her a hug and she pushed me away and said that she didn't like the smell of my perfume. And she asked me to park around the corner so that her friends don't have to see me when she gets dropped off because she needs to …

Susie   Appear to be independent and not need you.

Amelia   Yeah, so you know that is really bad, and her anger is, you know there was a crack in the door when she slammed the door on me last night after this row. But going back to your question about, you know, why is it? She has started stealing things and I don't know if that is normal. Is that normal?

Susie   What kind of things is she taking?

Amelia   Things of mine, like earrings. You know she will go into my underwear drawer … she has taken like a little silk slip I had – I mean what for? – so I don't know that kind of behaviour and I don't understand it, do you?

Susie   So on the one hand she is saying go away Mum, I don't want to be anything like you and I need to be my own person and you are so embarrassing, don't drop me near school, and at the same time she is trying to grow up and be her own person by taking your pretty underwear. It sounds like a confusion – so very common at this age: how can I be a young woman when I have got such a very powerful mum? Because to daughters all mums are very powerful.

Amelia   Oh.

Susie   And then how do I get her out of my life when I can't cross the road and I need her, while in fact I need the things that make *her* a woman.

I don't want to sound superficial, but just the way you have put it to me sounds like she is in a struggle to differentiate herself from you while still needing to have her hand held.

Amelia   Right.

I'm struck by how long and wordy my intervention is here. I'm aware that Amelia has been thrown by her daughter's turn from one day to the next, from darling girl to incomprehensible teenager, a category that has intensified over the last thirty years. There are many social and economic reasons for this, and the advent of social media has muddled the issues of belonging, of growing up, in different ways. Grace's teenage years have coincided with her absent father and Amelia's partner fading from family life. It's something I'd like to enquire about more in time. How does a family member's reduced presence affect the daughter and the mother?

Susie   She is kicking against you and yet still needing you.

Amelia   [*Pause*]

               You know it is really hard. I didn't want to bring her up
               in the way that I was brought up. I so wanted us to have
               a friendship and it has always been that. We have gone
               shopping together, she will make me listen to her latest
               music albums that she loves, and we have been to a rock
               concert together. We have done all of this great stuff
               together and now suddenly she doesn't want to at all.

Susie   She doesn't want you as a playmate any more.

Amelia   Right, yeah.

Susie   That's what you are saying.

Amelia   No, she doesn't.

Susie   She's sticking her hands up and going back off, or let me
               go forward without you in some way.

Amelia   Yeah.

Susie   And that is terribly hurtful for you.

Amelia   It feels quite …

Susie   A shock to your …

Amelia   It is a big shock, yeah, it is a big shock and, you know, I
               can't share it with David, my husband, because he is just
               not around, so you know I don't know, and I can't seem to,
               I just don't know how to negotiate.

               I don't know how to talk to her now, and also I am really
               sick with worry and haven't slept because I don't, I don't
               think this is, I don't know whether it is right or not, but I
               went through her messaging and I have found …

Susie   Which one, a public one or a private one?

Amelia	Her private messaging, on Facebook, and I found she is in communication with this guy who is, you know, who is at the mixed school down the road and he is, he is a couple of years above her and, um, and it is really quite, you know, it is quite shocking, it is very …
Susie	What is shocking about it?

I don't take up the issue of Amelia's reading Grace's private messaging on Facebook. Led by frustration, Grace has sought to understand and to know what's driving Grace. A therapist is not there to pass judgement in a simple sense on the rights or wrongs of this breach, although it may have salience at some point.

Amelia	Well, it's very sexual.
Susie	Is it explicit?
Amelia	It is explicit, yeah, and that's … I've … you know, it's the first time I have kind of had to, I have never, I don't quite know how to, I haven't confronted her with it and I don't know if I should and I don't know …
Susie	What is it you would be confronting her with if you were confronting her?
Amelia	Well, I think I'd, um, I suppose I worry about her safety.
Susie	In what sense?
Amelia	Well, he may be into drugs, he could be a really bad influence, he could be, you know …
	She doesn't … we've never really … I have never had a personal conversation with her properly about sex, and I mean I know that, I mean it is a whole area that I have no control over with her so, you know, I'm fearful that she is sort of throwing herself off the edge of a cliff and she

doesn't know what she is throwing herself into. Um, and I know that …

Susie   So how do you talk about boyfriends in general, in the house?

Amelia   Well, who's flirting with who, um, you know if she is going out on a Saturday night, which I let her do as long as she is back by ten, then I like to know who she is going with and what they are going to be doing and then I like to check what she is wearing, which of late has become another bone of contention. But, you know, this is, they have obviously, my sense is that they have had some intimacy of some kind and so she has lied about where she has been, she is lying. If I call her on the phone there's not, she just doesn't pick up so I can't get anywhere near her, and I worry about, you know, I worry about him because he is a lot older, he is …

Susie   He's two years older, he is doing his A-levels?

Amelia   Yeah, yeah. You know, so …

Susie   What I am struck by in what you say, is how difficult this is for you.

Amelia   Right, right.

Susie   And there is a confusion between your concern *for her* and how to reach *her*.

There is the fact that she's struggling to have her own private life and develop different kinds of friendships and explore and experiment, and be impossible and perhaps choose a boyfriend from the school you wouldn't have expected, and that's hard for you.

Amelia   Yes, and he's mixed race as well, so David wouldn't be pleased about that, so that is something that I have to sort of keep quiet about. I don't know, it's another thing to negotiate, I suppose.

Susie   Can I ask, what is this idea of yourself as an executive who is managing everything? What is it you are managing?

You are talking about the difficulties of a child growing up and moving away, and not being able to direct them entirely, but she has actually had a very long time living with you and with your values, and her experimenting with a boy from the other side of the tracks from your perspective, why isn't that interesting and something for her to be doing at this point?

Amelia   Oh, I suppose I hadn't thought of that. Yes, that's interesting.

Susie   Tell me about you as a teenager. What did you do that your parents just could not fathom?

Amelia   Um, well, my father was very frightening, so I obeyed, you know, it was a very, very different set of rules and it was a set of rules, and um, and that was difficult, so it was sort of, you know, a strict, a strict set of rules that you had to observe. I mean, one time when I was home late he, he, he held up a golf club against the guy that brought me home, so, and it was – you know, there are things that, I suppose – I suppose you are right, I suppose it is more about me because there are things that, you know, he, my father said that sex was dirty, for instance, so you know …

Susie   So did you dare to kiss and have …

Amelia   Yes, I did, yeah.

Amelia and Susie   [*Laughing together*]

Amelia   I did, I did. But why is it then that she is feeling this need if I've … it's interesting to me that you say I am managing her, because I feel as if I have been very liberal with her, and I have been her friend and now I'm, and she's been mine, and I'm losing my friendship.

Susie   You have been her mum actually, and you have been a particular kind of mum, and I think one of the difficult situations for parents is that children go through an aspect in their own development of disavowing their parents, but knowing that there is something a bit odd about that, so they and you remain close through the fighting. It is a way of kind of keeping close while keeping a certain distance.

Amelia's genuine interest in Grace's life – listening to the records she likes and so on – is admirable as has her desire to sculpt a different kind of mother–daughter relationship from the one she grew up in. Judging how close, how much 'friendship', how much what a child needs from a parent varies at different ages, is not straightforward, and for many the imprint from one's own history doesn't serve as a model to emulate. For Amelia it was one to contest. Rejecting authoritarianism doesn't mean jettisoning authority but working out how the dosages of guidance, authority, interest, boundaries and freedom change and, like many parents, Amelia is shaken up by the radical shift in Grace's way of being and she feels abandoned.

Amelia   Um.

Susie   There are bumps when kids grow up, as they grow up, they want and need different things from a parent.

Amelia   Yeah, I guess.

Susie   I am not wanting to minimise what you are feeling about your concerns, but I am also thinking, you said, she is so clever but she's not focused.

Amelia   But she doesn't have a direction.

Susie   She's sixteen.

Amelia's academic concerns for Grace have me wondering about
Amelia's ambitions for her: what are they? Do they include intellectual and artistic exploration, or does Amelia's take on the world
lead her to feel her daughter must set her sights now and work
towards excluding what might be surplus to those goals? Education
has veered between forced specialisations to a broader curricu-
lum, to mixing about sciences and arts subjects, to an emphasis on
STEM subjects. I'm wondering about whether Amelia isn't showing
similar concerns to the mothers of the women like Helen (p. 85),
who in wanting so much for their daughters may have inadvertently
sent signals about ambition and achievement that then bypassed
the pleasures of learning and exploring what might be right for the
person. So I'm eager to understand Amelia's frustration with her
daughter's unbounded cleverness.

Amelia   Yes, but it seems to me now that you have to have a
               very clear direction from quite a young age, you know,
               because even if you go to university now and come out
               with a double first, you can still end up working, you
               know, working a till somewhere. It doesn't guarantee you
               a future in the way that it used to, and I do not want her to
               go through that.

Susie   So you are frightened for her.

Amelia   An unfulfilled working experience in the way that, in the
               way that *I* have, I suppose. [*Long pause*]

               She has astonishing potential and um … [*Long pause*]

               I guess I just want her to be OK.

Susie   Yes, of course you want her to be OK, I was thinking about this bit and …

Amelia   Do you not think her behaviour is very extreme, though, I mean considering we are always going to fight?

Susie   I am afraid I don't actually. I don't think it's extreme for a London girl. I don't think keeping her options open because she is capable and can do anything is a problem; I think it's a plus. I can see what you are saying about kids who have got ambition and want to go down this line, but there is also something about living and exploring learning.

I think the fact that she is being dismissive is incredibly hurtful, but it is perhaps something about her own identity that she is exploring.

She has been such a great companion and you have been so close, I am not sure if it is the mixed-race young man, if it is the dirty room with the dirty clothes, the explicit texts or messaging but that is something that is happening for this generation, they are finding a different world, they live in a different world. It is a hell of a challenge for parents, and the forms of safety that you wanted to give her have to be rethought in a way.

The question is perhaps how do you have the conversation, as opposed to how do you put *your* fear in there, which then I imagine frightens her, or closes her down, which makes her think you just don't understand, and so she bangs the door.

Amelia   But do you not think it's … do you not think it's true that if you do have a more liberal relationship with your child, that it therefore, you know, you think in your head that that's going to create an environment that, or a safer environment for them, or one where they feel they can come and talk to you about anything, that's what I thought.

Susie   I think that is absolutely the case, but that doesn't also mean they don't need privacy.

Amelia   Right. Well, I mean, I don't know what to do.

Susie   Does she know you are worried about her?

Amelia   Yeah, I would have thought so, and I think she is in a hell of a state as well.

Susie   OK, does it make sense to you that I meet her?

Amelia   Oh God, right, OK. [*Laughing*] I don't know how I would get her in here, but yeah.

I'm picking up a lot of anxiety from Amelia and although I'm not particularly alarmed by what she is reporting, the relationship is saturated with tension and an inability to hear each other; hence my suggestion that I meet Grace.

Susie   I am not sure. I can't evaluate whether your worries are about being a mum in 2017 and the terrible experience of rupture that is occurring right now, or whether there is something much more serious going on, that you've picked up. Maybe I can get a sense of what that is myself.

Amelia   Oh yes, yes. I think that would be … I mean, from my point of view that would be marvellous.

Susie   So why don't we do that? But in the meantime I think it might be worth your thinking about the moments of struggle for your own privacy when you were her age, which of course weren't expressed through living on an iPhone …

Amelia   No, that's true.

Susie   … and weren't expressed by being rude to parents. And
                I also think you are very isolated with this, as you have
                said, and it would be important to find a way, I don't think
                we can do it just today, but to be able to talk with your
                husband about this. You know, he's not your dad, he is not
                going to hit the roof if you say this is what's going on.

Amelia   No he's not, but he's just not going to be interested
                because he's just, his focus is elsewhere.

Susie   OK, well, I am sorry, but we are going to stop for now.

Amelia   OK.

Susie   And I will see your daughter and we will take it from there,
                OK.

Amelia   Thank you very much Susie, thank you.

Susie   Alright, OK.

Amelia   Thanks.

Second Session (Grace)

Grace walks in, urchin-like, with a short haircut, blue jeans, grey Converse Hi Tops, an open face and a sassy feel to her.

Amelia	Hello Susie, this is Amelia, I am just dropping Grace off.
Susie	OK, come on up, Grace, all the way up to the top.
Amelia	There you go darling, push the door, harder, that's it.
Grace	You are going to come back here?
Amelia	Yeah, I'll meet you later.
Grace	OK, bye, wait here.
Susie	Grace, hi, I'm Susie.
Grace	Hi Susie.
Susie	Come on in.
Grace	Thanks.
Susie	Please take a seat on the sofa.
Grace	OK. I don't know what to do here really, sorry.
Susie	Well, what did Mum say to you?
Grace	She said, she said that she went and she did some therapy with you and she said it was helpful and she thought that I could gain something from it as well. We kind of had a fight about it but, um, I've come. I'm a little bit, I don't know, it's weird coming here and doing it because I don't know, I just kind of always thought just crazy people go to therapy.
Susie	Uh-huh.
Grace	And I'm not crazy, but, um, you know, I came, so I obviously wanted some sort of help, so I'm here.

Susie   So what, beyond having the fight about it, what did you think might be helpful to you?

Grace   Um, well that's kind of like a difficult question really because I almost think that this is more helpful to my mum, and I feel like if she does this then, she'll get off my back a lot more.

I think that she is super-unhappy about a lot of things and that kind of like puts pressure on me. I feel like she is trying to force this relationship with me, um, by just being like really overbearing.

She's always kind of in my face, and she wants me to do this, and she wants me to do the washing up, and she wants me to do the laundry, and she kind of says all these things thinking, oh, this is a connection with my daughter, oh, if I stop her from going out in the weekdays and on the weekends, if she comes home at six on the weekdays, then she is forced to spend some time with me, but actually it just stops me from enjoying spending my time with her because I am kind of forced to do it, like she is trying to force a friendship with me, um, um, and it is, I don't know, it is not like I don't want to be friends with my mum, but just the way that she is going about it. I think it is a little bit kind of desperate, and it puts a lot of pressure on me. I think that's because Dad has been away so, I don't know however long now really. I think she is trying to fill a void with me, thinking that she is looking after me and thinking that she is trying to make me not notice that Dad is not around, but ultimately I just kind of notice that she is the one that is really suffering from Dad not being here, I think. I don't know if that makes sense, but …

Susie   It does make some sense. How is it for you with your dad not being around?

Grace   Well it, it's hard in a lot of ways. Like I used to be really close to my dad, and now obviously that is not the case any more, and he used to – well, you know how parents play good cop and bad cop, and it felt like he was good cop and Mum was bad cop, and now that he's gone, I'm just left with bad cop, so that's …

Susie   When you say he's gone, does that mean he doesn't come home?

Grace   It feels like he is never home.

Susie   But what is the reality for you, when do you see him?

Grace   Um, so I'll see him come in and out, but I won't see him in terms of spending time with me, so we are really disconnected now. He is away on weekends, he's busy working during the week and he won't get home until really late, and, um, I have to be in bed by 10.30, so I don't get to see him, and when I do it's just 'Hey honey, got to go, love you, bye', which doesn't really feel like love, I guess.

Susie   Um, how long has that been going on?

Grace   Quite a few months now, I think it is like seven or eight months, in a year that is quite important because I've got my GCSEs now and I'm studying quite a lot, so it's like he's, it feels like he's sort of abandoned me and abandoned Mum and disappeared from us at quite a crucial time, like he doesn't want to put up with the pressure of being a dad at such an important time, I guess.

I'm interested in Grace's understanding of her dad: he doesn't want to put up with the pressure of being a dad at such an important time for her. As we shall see, she is pondering his absence for her and its meaning for her mum. She is showing a great deal of thoughtfulness and I feel drawn to her.

Grace   Like it makes me sad, because I feel it affects Mum more
              than it affects me.

Susie   Because it puts her on you or because …

Grace   Yeah, I think it puts her on me, thinking that she is being
              there for me but I think she is trying to be there for herself.
              Like, I wouldn't even be surprised if Dad was having an
              affair or something and, I don't know, I don't know if he is
              or whatever, but that is the kind of things that my friends
              tell me – oh it's typical, he's probably sleeping with the
              secretary, and things like that – and I don't know if Mum
              even feels that way. She is just forcing a relationship with
              me.

Susie   So before he disappeared or abandoned you in this way,
              how were things with you and your mum? I know you said
              she was the bad cop, but how did you get on even inside
              of that? Were you pretty close or not?

Grace   No, we were never close.

Susie   Uh-huh.

The starkness of Grace's response both surprises me and doesn't.
In therapy one is always listening to the individual's story and then
taking a beat to reflect on it. Is this accurate? Is anything missing?
What does it mean when someone heartbroken says they hate their
ex? We know that one part of them does and another part is hurt,
angry, confused, humiliated or pushing away a strong love because
it's too painful to show oneself how much one cares. Grace says she
was never close to her mum, and I'm thinking very few don't have a
strong attachment to a parent and so I'm keeping an open question
for myself about whether this isn't also a case of fierce repudiation
because Mum is infuriating her at present.

Grace   But it was easier when Dad was around. I don't know, easier in some ways but not in others, because they would argue a lot, but at least then I could go away and be in the shadows or whatever, and go away and be on my phone and not get involved, but now that he is not there, she is arguing with me. When he was around, he would do a lot of stuff with me and Mum is working hard, and she has got other things to focus on and she was like into her fitness and everything, so she would be around to tell me, OK, have you done your homework, OK, did you study for this, OK, have you done your laundry, which I get is obviously what a parent should do, but it takes the fun out of a mother–daughter relationship, but it was fine – I guess it is just kind of what a mother–daughter dynamic is really. I never hated her, and now I feel like I hate her sometimes, which I know that I don't but just the way that she goes about things makes me just hate her and almost feel sorry for her, but not necessarily even in a good way because I feel like she has got all this desperation for something. She is looking for something and I am the wrong person to be looking for it from – I am her daughter, you know, I feel like it is almost like I have to mother her.

Susie   Uh-huh.

Grace   Which is just backwards, so …

Grace is complaining that she needs to mother her mother. This is not uncommon. Still, in the vast majority of families, it is mothers who do the mothering, the hands-on day-to-day raising of their children, and in that scenario, in which a mother is thinking about what her child needs, what her partner needs, what her parents need, she might also feel and be emotionally neglected herself. It's not unusual for mothers to look to their daughters for emotional support and nurture. In a complex way it is part of the psychological upbringing of girls who are being introduced to the expectations of their future life, which will include care of others. Unconsciously a mother may prepare her by expecting her daughter to nurture her. Despite social changes in the past forty years, the internalisation of femininity still encodes nurture of others as critical to identity, and what Grace is telling us here is a version of struggling against becoming her mother's mother.

Susie   So if you could have it the way you would like it, what would it look like?

Grace   I would quite like to be able to see my friends, I just want it – I kind of want it to be like how my friends' relationships with their parents are. Like, my friends always seem to be hanging out with each other and going to the cinema and going to the park and hanging out and growing up, and I feel like I am being stopped from doing that, so like the ideal situation would be for me to, at the end of the school day, if my guys are going to the park, great, let's go hang out for a bit, cool, or I am going to go home now, it's getting kind of late, I would like to go home, rather than my mum forcing me to be home at a certain time.

You know, I feel, it's really annoying, I feel like my mum doesn't quite accept or understand or see that I'm, I'm not an idiot and I have values and I look after myself and I don't want to go down like a wrong path or whatever. I feel like she is probably scared that I am going to start doing drugs and going crazy, but I'm not, I'm not interested in that, all I'm interested in is having friends and having a social life outside of also studying and working hard, because it stops … when you are just doing that, it stops life from being fun. … Sorry, sorry, it's just the phone.

Susie   Won't you turn if off for the moment please?

Grace   Turn my phone off?

Susie   Yes, sessions are a phone-free zone.

Grace   I've got it on silent then it just vibrates, it doesn't buzz.

Susie   Yeah, but we just both got interrupted and it will irritate me I am afraid.

Grace   Oh, OK, I'll turn it off then, sorry. Where have I been asked to do that before, sorry. My mum always gets annoyed that I am on my phone. But the thing is that my social life is kind of on my phone now, because she, in the week, she says I have to be home by six and then on the weekends I have to be home by ten, so I don't actually have time to see my friends and have a real interactive …

Susie   Well, what do you think would be reasonable?

Grace   I think I should just be given freedom. I just think she needs to trust me, that's all, I don't feel like I need a curfew. She just doesn't understand me, she really doesn't understand me, I don't think she sees the capabilities of her daughter. I am taking eleven GCSEs, I don't even need to like revise that hard for them, because I'm, because I get it. Like, I'll concentrate in the classroom and it goes in, like it stays in my brain. I remember one time we had this mock exam coming up for history and I forgot that it was coming up, and so I got to school and they said OK, we've got this mock exam and I was like 'Oh my God', and then I did it and I ended up getting a B+ and it was totally fine. Obviously if I had revised I would have got an A, which is what I want, but it is just things like that where I don't think my mum gets *me*, because she is always like revise, revise, revise, you have to be home at six so you can revise, and so she doesn't actually see that her daughter is bright and able, and she can trust me, if she gives me a little bit of freedom, like she can trust me. That is why we are arguing all of the time, we just don't get each other, like 'cos she doesn't get me, I kind of refuse to get her, although I do empathise with her, but …

Susie   Are you able to say to her, Mum, I am actually responsible and I would like a bit more leeway, I do do my studies, and you don't need to worry about me so much?

Could you ever say that, as opposed to have a fight about it?

Grace   Yeah, that's what I was going to say. I feel like, I feel like I've shouted that at her like plenty of times but I haven't, um, said it.

[*Pause*]

Susie   Are there things that you are worried about, though, about yourself?

Grace   About myself?

I think I am worried about growing up, I guess, but I think all teenagers are scared about growing up really – it is quite a scary thought. Like, I am studying for lots of different subjects but I don't know which subjects I want to concentrate on, I don't know what I want my career to be, and I know that really frustrates my mum, she wants me – she thinks I'm not focused but …

Susie   OK, but let's try and talk about you, what do you …

Grace   Yeah, I know. That's what I mean, I just don't think I'm ready to move on to the next step, yet I am being forced to move on to the next step. I am scared about growing up because just everything seems so messed up, like it doesn't seem like an environment that I want to grow up in right now.

I just think the economy and the government, everything is just so messed up from your generation, from my mum's generation, that us as kids, we have to – us kids, us teenagers or whatever, the next generation – we have to actually clean up the mess that has been going on and it is a really big mess, and it is really intimidating the idea of growing up and going into that, you know, I am going to be basically like a – it is going to feel like I'm the street cleaner cleaning up the streets after you guys, and so Mum wants me to grow up but I don't want to grow up into her mess. Everything is so expensive now, I wouldn't be able to afford rent if I were to move out, so it is really hard because I do like the idea of being an adult, I really like the idea of being independent and not having to deal with my mum or my dad, but then also the thought of actually doing that is going to be terrifying.

Susie   That is a hell of a pressure though, Grace. You have got a good bit of time before you have to do that.

Grace   Yeah, well yeah, I almost sometimes get frustrated by education because I know it is a long time, but I almost prefer the idea of life being independent, so yeah, maybe I am putting that pressure on me, but don't all teenagers at this time when you are doing your GCSEs get scared and feel all of the pressure at this time of what is going to happen? I think that is why so many kids stay in education and do college and then do uni and stuff, because they are not ready to be in the big world.

Susie   Yes, I think that's true, but I don't think you go from one state to the next overnight. That is why there is this long apprenticeship to being a grown-up.

Grace   Yeah, that's true, yeah, yeah.

Susie   And of course the passion you feel about having to clear

up for your mum's generation is really understandable.
You have to remake the world and repair it from how you
found it. And you wish it weren't as it is.

Grace   Yeah.

Susie   But I'm not sure that's quite what's on your doorstep. I
think what's on your doorstep is the possibility of you
finding your way into making your own contribution
and finding what interests you. Otherwise it can be a bit
overwhelming.

Grace   Yeah, I think that could be right.

[*Long pause*]

Susie   What are you thinking?

Grace   Just [*long pause*] just thinking of the pressures Mum puts
on me, that's all.

Susie   To look after her, or to be a certain kind of person yourself?

Grace   Both of them really. And I guess the pressures that I am
kind of putting on myself.

Susie   Yeah.

Grace   Like, I made the choice to study eleven different GCSEs,
which is quite a lot, and I did that because I would like
options because I don't know what I want to do.

Susie   Uh-huh.

Grace   But then also I feel like I had to do that to please my mum
because I don't think she enjoys her work very much and
she wants to make sure that I do enjoy my work.

Susie   Well, are you enjoying the eleven GCSEs, because that is
your work now, isn't it?

Grace   Yeah, it is. It is not that I enjoy them – like, I can do them but It doesn't make me enjoy them.

Susie   And are there ones that you want to take forward?

Grace   There are ones that I like more than others. I really like drama and I like English, but I wouldn't know what to do with those, I don't think that those are areas that my parents would really like me to go into if I were to like pursue a career in drama or writing, so I have to keep my options open so that my mum thinks that I am going to maybe pursue something else and have a real job.

Susie   What does that mean? You mean you've got to take physics and further maths in order to please your mum, or have job possibilities?

Grace   Yeah, I think so. But also I have to take maths. I do feel like I do everything so that she could take me seriously, or that she could see I would have options later to choose from, but really what I want to do is something a bit more creative. My parents aren't creative people, so I think that sort of scares them.

Susie   So when you say you want to be creative, what does that mean when you say writing or drama?

Grace   It just means, like, expressing something, like, when I was younger I wrote some – like, I had these crazy dreams and I would write them down, almost like in those dream diary type things, but then I actually made them into little stories, and yeah, I would show them to Mum or whatever, they would be like, oh well done, and then sort of leave it on the counter and not really take an interest in it. Um, so I like stuff like that, I just, I like, I don't know how I want to express myself yet, but I know that I have things to express I think.

Susie	How is your English teacher?
Grace	Yeah, she's fine, she is quite encouraging. She took one piece of my homework that she really liked and she showed it to our headmistress, because she was that proud of it. And my headmistress like called me in and said well done, so that was really cool.
Susie	Was it that, was what was cool that somebody acknowledged your work?
Grace	Yeah.
Susie	Or they got that you were original or …
Grace	Yeah, basically just sort of saying, oh you can do it, you can do that, and that's, yeah, that's what's cool.
Susie	Uh-huh.
Grace	Because that's what sort of starts you thinking, oh OK, maybe I could, maybe I, maybe I should try more with that.
Susie	Uh-huh.
Grace	Maybe that's why I don't really study that hard for my other subjects, because I don't, really I don't have much of an interest in them, you know, I'll try to have an interest in them but they – my brain takes things in and I can do well in other subjects, but it is not necessary that I care about them.
Susie	Uh-huh. But what's interesting is that you are telling me how much you care about something whereas you didn't think you did.
Grace	Yeah, I guess that's true.
Susie	I mean you care about wanting to hang out with your friends, you care about writing and expressing yourself.

Grace   Yeah.

Susie   You obviously care about your mum because you wouldn't feel so burdened by having to look after her, even though it would be good if you didn't have to do that, and it sounds like you miss your dad a lot, or you don't know how to connect, so you really care about the change there, so you don't sound at all unfocused to me.

Grace   Maybe you should tell my mum that, she doesn't think so.

I haven't really thought about it like that, I just kind of ignore things.

Susie   Yeah, I think it is a lot to ask, but what would it be like if, when she's giving you a hard time, you didn't engage at that level and you just said yes I hear you Mum and I'm doing those things, you know whatever the demand she's making on you – what would that be like?

Grace   I think that would, well, it would be really hard, but it would be almost like not entertaining her argument so maybe she would. She would maybe calm down as well and we could have a talk about it instead. Yeah, I guess it would be helpful, but it is just really hard.

Susie   Uh-huh.

It's a pleasure to see the way Grace's mind works and the flexibility she has to think her way around the clash she is in.

Grace   When someone comes in at you, like, with all these sort of accusations that you're not working hard enough and you're not focused, all you want to do is defend yourself and tell her to shut up.

Susie   Well, I suppose she feels worried and concerned for you, and you get her anxiety about you, so that stops you saying, actually Mum, I am quite scared about growing up but there are things that really interest me, and you then lose out on having the conversation, don't you?

Grace   Yeah.

Susie   I don't think it is easy for you to lead it but …

Grace   Yeah, it's like we never get there.

Susie   Yeah, you just sort of have a proxy conversation in terms of a row.

Grace   Yeah, I think that's true.

Susie   Well, look, let me have a think about what I think might be right between you and Mum and whether you come together or …

Grace   OK.

Susie   And you can let me know also how this settles in for you.

Grace   Yeah, OK.

Susie   OK.

Grace   Yeah. Alright. Thank you Susie. Can I turn my phone back on now?

Susie   Of course.

As we end the session, I'm holding several strands. There is Amelia's concern about her daughter. There is Grace's wanting to push her mother off and repudiate her. There's Dad's absence, Grace's concerns about having to remake our environment and how she's ever going to grow up. There is also the issue of loss, of developing sexuality, of class and race issues and the fact that both Amelia and Grace are closing the door on each other while needing to renegotiate their relationship. In the next session the three of us meet together.

Third Session (Amelia and Grace)

It is ten days later, and I'm curious about how each of them has absorbed what was talked about. I had a hopeful feel about the two of them sorting things out in time. In this session I am interested to see how they do relate and to see if we can see how the sore spots can be addressed differently.

Susie   Hello.

Amelia   Hello, it's Amelia.

Susie   Come on up.

Amelia   Thank you.

Susie   Hello.

Amelia   Hello, I'm so sorry she's not here.

Susie   Well, you are a couple of minutes early.

Amelia   I'm early, am I? Well, OK. Well, I mean, she said, I said meet, I said meet me on the doorstep at ten to four, she is coming from school, but you know, she is not here, so anyway, um, the anxiety is that, you know, she has to pass the other school so maybe she has met up with um what's his name, anyway, so I am really sorry ... You know, I hate

...

[*Doorbell*]

Susie   There she is.

Amelia   OK, right.

Susie   Hello.

Grace   Hi Susie, it's ...

Susie	Come on up.
Grace	Thanks. [*Climbs stairs quickly*] Hi Susie, I'm sorry I'm a bit late, I was waiting for …
Amelia	[*Said with edge and fury*] Where have you been?
Grace	You are already here!
Amelia	Yes, I'm already here.
Grace	Are you kidding me? [*Raises her voice*]
Amelia	We agreed to meet at ten to four, and why is your phone off?
Grace	I have literally just been stood on the street for ten, fifteen minutes waiting for you. You told me to meet there on the corner.
Amelia	No I didn't, I said to meet here, at the door here.
Grace	Everyone finished school and they were just going past me and going past me, looking at me like some idiot.
Amelia	Why is your phone switched off?
Grace	It's not switched off, I have been using it to …
Amelia	Well, why don't you answer me when I texted you?
Grace	It has no battery, Mum. I didn't turn it off, I didn't switch it off.
Amelia	OK, so I said ten to four here, and you weren't here.
Grace	Well, at ten to four I was up on the corner like you told me to be on the corner, and then I've just been running down here because I don't want to be late for Susie, and you are already here. Don't tell me the corner if you don't mean the corner Mum.

Amelia   I had to come in because it is rude not to.

Grace   Yeah, exactly, that's why I ran down the street because it is rude not to.

Amelia   It's alright, shush now.

Susie   OK, could you both take a seat.

Grace   I am out of breath with all the running now.

Amelia   Oh dear.

Grace   OK.

Susie   Maybe it's useful that you've had the kind of fight that you have both told me about, but you've had it here and you've got two different stories.

Grace   It's not me this time.

Amelia   Who is it, your boyfriend?

Grace   I don't have a boyfriend, I don't know what you mean.

Amelia   Don't you?

Grace   I know you went through my Facebook, Mum, and Jevon is not my boyfriend, OK. Now are you going to trust me or not?

Amelia   Why would I trust you? Why *would* I trust you, having read that?

Grace   Yes, you read something, OK, we had a conversation, OK fine, it's not like anything has happened, I am not going out with him, I haven't been on a date with him. You never let me out of the house.

Amelia   I do let you out of the house.

Grace   Mum, you hardly let me out of my house.

Amelia   I let you out of the house, I absolutely let you. Yes I read
              your Facebook because – I've never done it before.

Grace   [*Little laugh*]

Amelia   I've never done it before.

Grace   And why should I believe you?

Amelia   But you are being so secretive, you are being so strange,
              you are lying to me all the time.

Grace   What am I doing that's secretive? How am I lying? I never
              lie to you, I don't. I've got nothing to lie about.

Amelia   Grace, you're stealing things from me.

Grace   That's not lying to you. You never asked me if I'm stealing
              and I said no. It's not even a big deal anyway. I don't steal
              that much. It started with – like, to be honest Mum – your
              lunches can be pretty terrible so sometimes I took a
              tenner from your purse so yes, I can get a better lunch,
              and then it became something else.

We are in the midst of accusation and counter accusation – 'why
should I trust you?', 'why should I trust *you*?' At the same time I'm
intrigued by what the stealing 'became something else' means but
we don't have time to know what that is just now.

Amelia   Well, why has my food suddenly become so repugnant to
              you? You've eaten it for sixteen years.

Grace   Yeah, it's pretty bland though, Mum. Also I want to change
              my diet a bit.

Amelia   Why do you want to change your diet?

Grace   Because.

Amelia	What's wrong with the diet? What's wrong with what you eat?
Grace	Because I don't want to eat animals.
Amelia	Oh my God.
	[*Sighing, exasperated*]
Grace	See that? She doesn't take me seriously. That is why I haven't told you. I don't …
Amelia	Is this something else Jevon has kind of …, you know?
Grace	Oh my God, it's got nothing to do with him.
Amelia	Do you Facebook about not eating cows?
Grace	No, we don't Facebook about not eating cows. You are just being ridiculous.
Amelia	You need, you have …
Grace	You're actually being childish now, that's a childish remark.
Amelia	I mean, I don't know where to go when you have absolutely no respect for me whatsoever, it is just impossible.
Susie	Is there another way of thinking about this, Amelia? When we talked, it seemed to me that Grace is trying to express herself, she is trying to grow up a little bit.
Amelia	Um um, yeah.
Susie	And part of growing up, Grace, is saying to Mum, 'I want to change what I eat' or 'I would like a bit of privacy'. For you, Amelia, that might feel like a rejection, rather than you considering that Grace is developing her own ideas and her own opinions and her own direction. I believe she is testing things out and needs you to respond in a way that says 'Oh that's interesting'.

Amelia   Yes.

Susie   I'm not sure it *is* as rejecting as you think.

Amelia   Well, I suppose I could get my head around the idea that,
               you know, that you are needing to try new things, but the,
               the attitude and the velocity of, of, of the force that goes
               behind it, it is just – and the fury, is, is just not what I feel
               has been the way we have conducted our relationship in
               the past, and it makes it impossible for me to … some of
               the time it makes it impossible for me to even hear what
               you are saying because of the foulness with which you are
               saying it, you know.

Grace   I don't think that's totally fair because I think that you
               speak to me similarly.

               [*Pause*]

Susie   You both see the other as so incredibly powerful that
               you've got to either impose or push away one another
               with incredible force. Just as in that argument. What I
               heard or saw was a hurt that neither of you is being heard
               by the other. You would like to protect your daughter and
               help her on her way, but Grace would also like you to hear
               that she is a responsible young woman you could trust.

Amelia   Yes, but I haven't …

Susie   And Grace is saying that she's doing some different
               things now, that are about being sixteen, or anticipating
               going forward. There is something quite shared in your
               experiences that you think she is a very powerful girl and
               she thinks you are a very powerful mother, and of course
               you are both having an enormous impact on each other.

               There is something that is not being shared that could
               be shared. Grace is saying I am trying to do things a bit
               differently and you, Amelia, are not seeing that. You don't

want the aggression, I get that, but if you were able to give a bit more space.

Amelia   Yeah, it's hard to do that though because, because it is difficult to trust you, it is because you are being so secretive and dishonest, and if, if we could sit down at a table and be a bit more open with each other in a kinder way maybe … I mean I, I, I hear what you are saying, Susie, I do.

Susie   Your feeling, Amelia, is that Grace is rejecting you, she is being dishonest, she is being secretive. Is there another way for you to see that she is trying to develop a little bit and she is trying to separate a bit, and she hasn't known how to tell you that she has gone, or considering being, a vegan or a vegetarian.

Amelia   You mean she doesn't? [*Looks quizzically*]

Susie   Doesn't know how to tell you things.

Amelia   Right. Doesn't know how to tell me things, yes.

[*Pause*]

Susie   Well, because mothers are very powerful to go up against. Even for the loveliest, kindest, most benevolent mums, it can feel like a very big thing for a daughter.

Amelia   You mean so it is not a deliberate sort of um, ah, act of, kind of, well sort of …

I sort of see it as total, you know, as very rejecting, I suppose, and um, you know, I'm not sure why because I'm not sure if I've invited that.

Susie   But shall we find out if it is that and what your intention is. Grace, can you try and say something?

Grace   It kind of makes me sad that that's how you look at it and how you take it. I think Susie's right, that's not what I'm trying to do. I am not trying to just reject you, I just want to be able to try new things, experience things, be a teenager that's becoming an older teenager, or an adult or whatever, and I feel like you stop me from doing that, and then I guess I act out in the wrong ways thinking that will fix it, or stop you from making me do certain things. I don't know if that makes sense. I'm not rejecting *you*, but the way that you go about things. The way that I fight against you I can see could come across like I'm rejecting you, but I'm not.

Susie   Can you imagine a way that your mum could hear you?

In this session I'm listening for what Grace finds difficult. I'm also listening to see whether Amelia's fear that Grace is going off the rails is occurring. Grace feels impinged upon, and her response is to shut off in such a way that she sucks up the airspace and mother and daughter do a belligerent dance together.

Grace   Yeah, I know we kind of talked about it before, but I know that when we start talking about something, we actually end up arguing rather than entering into a conversation on a conversational level. We enter everything with emotion and aggression or tears, or whatever, so neither one of us ever gets heard. Susie and I spoke about approaching it differently, which I think we both need to do.

Susie   Can you imagine from your side, Amelia, being interested in what your daughter has to say instead of being frightened about what is going on?

Amelia   Um, yeah, actually.

                    Um, I suppose it means renegotiating, you know, it means renegotiating who we are with each other, doesn't it?

Susie   Uh-huh.

Amelia   Um, it's a difficult, it's a difficult adjustment, isn't it, the idea that you can't, you can't, you can no longer, you know that I can't, it feels very weird to me, I don't know.

Susie   Well, it is weird because – you've produced a lovely young woman but she wants you to get to know her as a young woman, and I think she wants something different from you. She is probably not as interested in you as you are interested in her because that is the way of it, but I think she is saying I would like to see another bit of my mum.

Grace   Yeah, I want you to know that it's not like I don't want to be friends with you.

Amelia   Thanks. [*Amelia and Grace laughing*] I mean that's good to know, you know.

Grace   I get that right now it's hard for both of us with Dad, he's obviously away a lot, and so me and you are in each other's company a lot and, um, I know that that is hard, and also I am at the age where things change. Oh God, I feel really embarrassed saying this, but I am legally allowed to have sex, maybe I shouldn't have said that, but I just mean like this conversation with …

Amelia   Yeah, but the thing is, the thing is that …

Susie   If you can listen, Amelia, Grace is talking to you.

Amelia   Right, OK.

Grace   So I just mean, so this conversation with Jevon – like, I know as a mum, well, firstly, you shouldn't have read it, but secondly, as a mum who has read it, I know that that's not nice to read because it got flirty or whatever, fine, I get that, but also I feel like I'm allowed to. At some point I am going to be interested in boys, and at some point I will have a boyfriend and he will, you know, come home and he'll meet you or whatever, and I don't feel like I should feel bad about doing that. Nothing happened with Jevon, I don't fancy Jevon or anything like that, you know. I'm not planning on, you know, dating him or whatever, but I just mean I want to feel allowed to be able to grow up, you know, I feel at that stage, and I'm not an idiot Mum, I'm not stupid, I have values and I feel that those don't get appreciated by you, I don't think you see …

Amelia   Well, I helped create the values, but yeah.

Grace   That's what I mean, I don't think that you see the daughter that you have raised. I'm not, I'm not an idiot and I'm not going to just, you know, I'm not going to mess about with the wrong kind of people and I'm not going to just sleep around like I'm just …

I'm interested in growing up, like you did. Like you're a grown-up now, you've had me.

Amelia   I know that, I know that. I know how clever you are, I know how talented you are, I know how beautiful you are, I know all of these things, I see them every day, but you don't necessarily know the influences of the world out there, you don't know …

Susie   Well, can we wait a minute – can we just take a pause there?

Amelia   Yep.

Susie   Because I think your daughter was asking you to hear something.

Amelia   Um, um.

Susie   And you have lots of wisdom to impart, but it's in how you deliver it that is going to be either useful or not heard, and thus going to produce this missing or connecting each other.

Amelia But how do you, you know… because, the thing is, I understand what you are saying, I do, but you are still living in a shared home which is a family home.

Susie But that's a different sort of story, isn't it?

Amelia Well, not really in that …

Susie You have every right to expect your daughter to be polite and keep her room to a certain standard, it probably won't be your standard but it …

Grace Does that mean that you think while I'm living at home I'm not allowed to have a boyfriend?

Amelia No, it doesn't mean that, but I … but I feel as if you haven't – I feel as if you have stopped respecting your environment and me in the environment, in the shared environment, you know.

Grace Like how?

Amelia Well if – we go through this on a daily basis, that your, your, you know …

Grace You mean because my room has been untidy for the last two weeks, you mean like that?

Amelia Well, filthy, but that's not quite what I'm saying. I'm saying that if I can, you know, I understand, I do understand what you're saying, Susie, I do understand that there are, there are freedoms that you need and I'm beginning to see that, but I'm also saying to you that you're still living at home and you're actually not …

Grace Free.

Amelia   No, you're not, and you're not quite an adult yet.

Amelia's tone is parental and controlled and also caring. She has softened her attack.

Grace   But that's not even what I'm saying. I know that I'm not an adult, I know that I don't pay rent, I know that I don't have a job, but at the moment all I am trying to say is it feels like you are not letting me go to the next stage.

[*Pause*]

Amelia   Uh-huh, OK, maybe that's, maybe you're right.

[*Pause*]

It's just so, it's so horrible and difficult when your child starts teaching you things.

[*All laugh*]

It is very strange.

Susie   Yeah, it is very strange, but it is a different basis for respect both ways, and what a wonderful thing to get from your child.

Amelia   Ummm.

Susie   And for your mum to recognise that.

Grace   Yeah, makes me really happy now we've had this chat.

Amelia   Do I need to listen to you more? Is that what I need to do?

Grace   Um, I think we both need to listen to each other more, but I think that right now, I think that my social life is like really restricted and I think I need to be off the leash a little bit more, because my friends get to, you know, hang out with each other after school quite a lot and I don't really get to do that, and I just … I would like to be able to do that.

Susie	Well, look, can we come back again when you've both thought about where you could both give in this specific arena?
Grace	Yeah, write a list, check it twice. OK.
Amelia	That colour of nails doesn't go with your uniform that well.
Grace	I get enough of that from my teachers, are you kidding? It's your nail polish. [*Laughing*]
Susie	OK, I'm sending you away.
Grace	OK.
Amelia	Thank you.
Susie	Alright.

Amelia and Grace's struggles are not uncommon. Amelia has laboured, emotionally and physically, to bring up Grace. She has nurtured her, introduced her to the world, to what it means to be a girl and fit in with the mores of her social, ethnic and class position. In the way that she has been with Grace and with Grace's father she has given Grace an emotional repertoire about how relationships go along, and Grace will have absorbed how horizontal relationships between parents work (or don't), how this mother and father relate to her and so on. Grace's struggle to be her own person, with the right to express her own mind, exquisitely shows the teetering between boldness and uncertainty that besets adolescence. As Amelia tries to hold on to friendship, Grace is asserting that, while she still wants to be friends, they are mother and daughter and that this relation needs to be reconfigured.

Amelia's concern about Grace and social media is, again, not uncommon. Each generation of teenagers (since the invention of the teenager) have found ways to exclude their parents and the older generation as they forge their pre-adult identities. Once it was clandestine music listened to on a radio under the pillow, then it was dancing in overtly sexual ways, being on the phone for hours, using cannabis and MDMA etc. Such pursuits find expression with the smart phone. Its rapid communication connects the individual with virtual communities and friendship groups. The language and images shared and created for social media are alien to the parents, and this is part of the point: to be able to imagine a separate existence from one's family while being intensely connected to one's peers. The dependency switches from Mum and family to friends.

Adults are concerned about this not necessarily because they want to restrain their children per se but because the 'big bad world' which they have survived has become bigger (or is it smaller?) and more precarious. No parent doesn't know about sexting, the circulation of pornographic images of the young, the online grooming, the pressure girls feel to show explicit pictures of themselves, cyber-bullying and so on. The search for identity, recognition and appreciation outside the family can trump common sense and make a parent fearful. What Amelia has read in the texts between Jevon and Grace startles her. It wasn't done like that when she was young.

And there is Amelia's personal predicament. What constitutes a life for her when her daughter is trying to avoid her and her husband has all but left home? This is a challenging time for a mother not because of a tired cliché of the empty nest – although of course that has truth – but because she is looking at her daughter's opportunities and wondering about how to activate herself. What will be useful to her, and to Grace, will be for her to find things that absorb and satisfy her. The experience for a daughter of a mother continuing to grow is enormously useful. It cuts through guilt all around, but more importantly it is generative for Amelia to have a focus outside of the family.

Transitions in the mother–daughter, mother–child relationship are inevitable. As the child grows up, she or he needs very different things, and although a teenager's behaviour can feel like a repudiation, there is always a significant attachment and a desire for parental appreciation. It's the job of a parent to manage the rejection they feel inside of themselves without believing that it is a permanent state of affairs.

Harriet

I've been seeing Harriet for six months. She has recently separated from her long-term partner and has moved out of their shared home.

Harriet came to the UK from Zimbabwe when she was a little girl. She works in a primary school as the school secretary. She comes in bundled up from the cold, a maroon and yellow swirly scarf, nearly as big as her, wrapped around her neck and covering her dark blue coat. She feels very small as she sits forward in the middle of the sofa.

There aren't many words in the session, but it feels to me as though we are connected through the active quiet we hold together. We are not at a loss with each other, or separated by the quiet. The quiet is full of feelings, which the session explores.

Susie   Hello.

Harriet   I'm a bit slow to get started these days. I'm sorry to have been late.

           God it's cold. I'm just going to be still for a moment, is that OK? …

           [*Long pause*]

           I feel as if I don't know why I am here today.

My pause matches hers.

Susie   Uh-huh.

Harriet   Well, I feel as if I could have – no, I was thinking about not turning up, but then – oh sod it, yeah, I thought, it's too late to change my mind. I made the commitment … [*Wry laugh*]

           How was your Christmas?

Susie   Tell me about yours.

Harriet   Quiet, it was quiet.

               I didn't want anyone around me, but my sister and my nephew came on Christmas Eve. That was lovely, it was good.

               And then there was a point when I really wanted them to go.

Susie   Uh-huh.

Harriet   Yeah.

               [*Long pause*]

Susie   Because you needed to return to and be with yourself?

Harriet   Yeah.

               [*Pause*]

Susie   Sad … or maybe depleted?

Harriet   Of course.

               [*Pause*]

               Everything has changed.

               Everything has changed so much in such a short time.

               I wanted to be on my own. That was good, that was good. That was right.

               I *am* on my own for the first time in such a long time, and the idea of trying to show face, keep up, seem all Christmassy jolly … no. I couldn't. I didn't want to do it.

               I did have invites, and that was lovely. I was pleased about that …

               Sorry – sorry, sorry, sorry.

I don't know what Harriet is saying sorry for, but I sense that if I ask I will be interrupting.

Harriet   Oh, and I hate saying sorry all the time, I hate saying sorry.

[*Long pause*]

How did I get here? That's what I have been thinking about the last few weeks, Susie. I'm haunted by a sense that one makes a decision and then a path opens up from that decision.

Everything I have been born with, grown up with, aspirations, hopes, oh … it's all gone askew …

It sounds so naff doesn't it, it sounds so naff.

The words aren't conveying the emotional dejection Harriet is transmitting, so I try to give her some.

Susie   You are heartbroken, and bewildered, and lost, and it is going to hurt like hell and be incredibly confusing.

Harriet   [*Crying with desperation*] How long is it going to take, how long is it going to take?

Harriet is in shock. She is slowly trying to assimilate a loss, a loss that can't find a place in her mind. A loss that doesn't want to be true. She doesn't know how she got to where she is. She is in a state of grief where it is hard for her to be with people and genuinely present for more than a few minutes.

Harriet needs to be heard, by which I mean she needs her experience validated by herself and by me. She's aching to be understood so that she can understand herself and what has happened. She needs somebody with her who can bear to go into the horror and the bleakness she feels. Her sorrow touches me deeply.

Harriet   I don't understand what I did wrong, I don't understand. Maybe I took too long trying to have a child, maybe I took too long, maybe I enjoyed myself too much.

I am forty-six years old and I don't understand what on earth is going on.

If you had asked me ten years ago, everything was brilliant. I could see, I could see forward, right now everything is just … [*Pause*]

Susie   Well, things are blocked and frozen.

Harriet   I don't understand how to get out of it. I don't like this feeling.

Susie   Tell me, what is this feeling, because when I said blocked and frozen, you put your hand in front of your mouth?

I'm always observing and, at the same time, almost experiencing a modified version of what the person I am working with is conveying.

In order to be with Harriet in the pain she finds herself in, I take on, in a minuscule way, for the time we are together, the flavour of her pain. This is a form of empathic identification which inevitably occurs for the therapist.

Being a therapist is a peculiar activity because a part of oneself is highly emotionally open, almost relaxed, as one reflects on what is being said and how it is being said and the way in which feelings are expressed. Simultaneously, we are feeling ourselves in our patients' shoes as we dwell with them in their pain and confusions and so, without knowing it, I have noticed Harriet's hand in front of her mouth. A part of me recognises the conflict she's experiencing between wanting to express herself and wanting to stop her words.

My question to her about her hand in front of her mouth is thus not thought out, it is spontaneous and curious.

Her physical presence in the session is characterised by a kind of folding in on herself. She looks quite tiny sitting on the sofa, but she isn't a small woman. The image that comes to me is that of a hibernating dormouse: hiding herself away until she can emerge from her frozen winter. When I tell her about her hand gesture, she looks up at me.

Harriet [*A little laugh*] I can see that, now you have pointed it out. I am very aware that I do that now, because I feel if I don't hold it back, it is going to be an avalanche.

It is going to be huge, and I am scared of that.

Harriet fears being overwhelmed. On the one hand she needs stillness, and on the other she needs words around her experience and the devastation she is feeling.

Harriet and her partner had had two rounds of IVF. They were both unsuccessful, and she left the home they had lived in together for six years.

Susie You didn't know that you weren't able to conceive.

Harriet No.

Susie In facing that, in coming to terms with that, the theft of a future, the theft of being able to carry a baby …

Harriet [*Sobs*] What do I do?

Susie Well, it's a double loss isn't it, Harriet, because you are dealing with the loss of your partner too, so you are very much at sea.

I don't address Harriet's question directly. I know that it is unanswerable. My job is to find a way to help her live through this anguish.

People wonder how something unbearable and unanswerable moves to become accepted, albeit a bumpy accepted.

What therapists observe in their practice is that, the more space there is for the expression of the complex feelings that such an event throws up, the more the capacity for mourning and loss can occur.

Loss is not a full stop. It is important to recognise and experience because in time the loss itself can move from being a present terror to a sadness that can be lived with. Outside the therapy room, people may wish to jolly Harriet along, or avoid her pain or be extra careful not to bring up the loss she has experienced. This is all done out of compassion and caring, but it hasn't helped, and doesn't help, Harriet.

Harriet	But I am not the only one, I know it happens to so many people, I know that, and I wasn't stupid going into it, the treatment, I wasn't stupid, but God I was hopeful.
Susie	Ah … ah.
Harriet	So I am finding it very hard to look at you today.
Susie	Uh-huh.
Harriet	How do you think I am doing in terms of managing all of this? It's not strange, is it?
Susie	I think it is very strange for you to find yourself in this situation and very painful, and also I don't know if there is some sense of shame that you are carrying.
Harriet	… yes, I do feel terrible shame …

It is almost like I was smelling shame. People communicate the subtlety of their feelings, and therapists are trained to catch them. It was only a whisper, but it came through to me. The clinical situation with its frame-by-frame speed slows down and reveals what otherwise can go unheard, unseen or unfelt. And so it was with Harriet's shame.

I think about her shame as being injurious to her sense of self. It is as though the shame comes in to protect her from the hurt that is in every one of her pores.

When you are drenched in shame, it stops other kinds of thinking and feeling. You are in a closed loop where it is hard to release the sorrow. But what will allow Harriet to live with meaning beyond this loss will be an ability to experience and then digest her pain, not be defended against it by shame.

Feelings are central to the work of psychological change. Feelings seem so ordinary and yet they can give us the biggest problems if we can't engage with them. When we misperceive what we feel, which Harriet experiences as shame, which can easily be stimulated and which doesn't seem to dissipate, then we might ask, is shame a 'cover' feeling as we saw with Douglas and anger – a feeling that the individual is accustomed to experiencing, ever available to be stirred up and yet one that, once felt, fails to relieve the individual. If we probe, we may be able to enable a wider spectrum of feelings, such as disappointment, sadness, hurt, loneliness, fragility. Such feelings, once experienced, may move the individual who is 'stuck'. Enabling and receiving the complexity of feelings and tuning into them accurately allows them to change as much as interpreting unconscious ideas.

Susie   It was a sense I felt when you said you couldn't look at me, and I was trying to understand the difficulty of you seeing me see your pain.

The tough thing is you just didn't get pregnant, and *that* you are not responsible for.

It is just absolutely awful, and I think it can be quite difficult to hold onto that awfulness and so you might go into shame, or it's my fault, when it just is.

Harriet   [*Crying*] It *is* my fault, I am forty-six years old and I don't know whether I can afford to pay you next time and I can't – I don't know where I am going to be living in the next week – I don't understand; how did I get here?

And I don't want to be a victim, I don't feel as if …

Susie   OK, so you are in a really bad spot. You chose to leave. You did it in a way …

Harriet's shame has closed her thinking down. She's shamed by the idea of being a victim, of being poor, of being in an unstable housing situation. She's alone. She's isolating herself and she's stuck.

Harriet   I couldn't stay.

Susie   OK, you couldn't stay, but actually that was also your home.

Harriet   Oh, it was too sad, it was too sad, it was too sad. I couldn't bear myself around him. He never got angry, he never got angry. Waiting to see his sadness was so overwhelming. His sadness was so overwhelming.

I am thinking about how his pain was unbearable for Harriet because it also augmented her own pain, but, knowing some of her background, I am also thinking of a curious parallel experience which she has enacted from her earlier life.

She left her partner after six years, following the failure of the second round of IVF. This mirrors an earlier departure when she came to the UK from southern Africa with her mother at the age of six. Her father stayed behind. This leads me to reflect on departures, and the suddenness of a rupture, and the impossibility for her of feeling she has the power to remake her relationship. She has exiled herself from her flat, from her partner with whom she suffered the loss of the promise of a baby and hence the future they had envisioned.

Harriet   This feels like an indulgence.

Susie   Uh-huh, but you know what comes across as so poignant is the two of you sobbing inside in your deep anguish but not able to speak.

When your dream collapsed, you both went into a silo, or you went into a silo. The hurt caused you shame and that makes sense of why you can't really be around people for very much time now.

I'm trying to get a counter-rhythm into the flow between us. Not to stop Harriet's horror but to play another tune alongside it. A tune that interrupts the doomed, inevitable, closed-down quality of the decision she made to leave her flat and partner.

Harriet   Yeah.

Susie   And I wonder whether you also feel an embarrassment that you don't think you can pay to come.

Harriet   That's my point. I need to come but I have so little.

Susie   That you feel that you don't have things to give.

Harriet   I don't. I feel awful about that … I can't believe right now … I don't know how I am going to balance things in the next month, that's the reason I didn't think I was going to come today, but then I went, well, you've booked in, you have to pay, if you don't go you still have to pay.

Susie   You made a certain set of choices in extremis, didn't you,
            and now you are thinking about those and their impact
            on you.

Harriet   Yeah.

Susie   And one of those is financial. It's not the only thing, but I
            think maybe it *is* time to reconsider. That's what you say:
            How did I get there, how did I do this, how did this happen?
            That's what we are looking at, and I think we will have to
            just put the finance bit between us on the side for the
            moment.

Harriet   I don't want to be owing, I don't want to be beholden.

Susie   No, I wouldn't do it that way. I don't think that would work.
            We need to agree that there is an amount that you could
            manage, and that is what you will pay because I also don't
            want you to be in an owing situation, I don't think that
            would be right.

Harriet   [*Whispering*] Thank you, thank you.

Susie   Will you think about what is plausible, honestly?

Harriet   Honestly I will.

Susie   And I will see you next Tuesday.

Harriet   OK.

I am thinking about how things that are incomprehensible can
make an individual feel quite helpless and the psyche doesn't like
feeling helpless. We would rather make ourselves responsible; we
would rather change everything around to make ourselves the
centre of our own misfortune. That then becomes a way of understanding. It also is the magical lever used in everyday thought, *if*

only I'd never started, I wouldn't be... if only I'd studied I could have got an A ...

We can either find that we blame ourselves or we can blame others and see things as their fault. Both those propositions keep people stuck.

Therapy can sidestep these two positions. It's a place to explore all the losses, the things gone wrong, the long-held anguishes, but it is not a place just to hide. It is a place to lift off the blame to see how Harriet has handled what has occurred. It is a place for her to think and feel whether she has more options than the shamed sorry-ness.

In time it will be a place for her to re-engage with her relationship with her boyfriend and to see whether she and he want to remake it. To see, too, whether the abruptness of the departure which was driven by the horror of the pain she felt herself and saw in her partner can be managed differently. And to consider whether her leaving was a kind of imprint from her childhood separation; a behaviour which she can now give up.

The sadness may not disappear, but it is something they both experienced and perhaps can support each other through. They wanted to make a family together. That desire was an expression of their love. Remaking that love in the face of their shared and separate loss could be a part of a deep, renewed, coming together again.

Harriet's departure from Zimbabwe was not something she could understand. She was a little girl who obviously wasn't in control of it and not much was explained to her. She lost the smell of her early childhood. She lost the scenery of her childhood. She lost the customs of the town she came from. She lost her extended family. She lost contact with her father too. I'm aware of the way she phrases things: *How did I get here? And that's what I have been thinking about the last few weeks, that sense that one makes a decision and then a path opens up from that decision.* She also says *I don't understand what I did wrong, I don't understand.* These words strike me as the sense of bewilderment that accompanied part of her childhood: *How did I get here? I don't understand what I did wrong, I don't understand.* They are a refrain of incomprehension, of what could not and cannot be explained.

Harriet's sense of helplessness is an example of a phenomenon we humans struggle with. We don't like to be helpless. And yet her sense of being helpless is real and psychically accurate. It throws her back to an early helplessness, also real but unexplained. To a six-year-old, that must have seemed inexplicable. So her feeling of helplessness is not a neurotic feeling to run away from. It is a difficult feeling to accept. But acceptance is what will in time help.

Much of the time we want to order and classify our world. We plan and strategise. We analyse and we count. We find comfort in binaries such as good or bad, excluded or included, friend or foe, right or wrong. Cultures vary in what is designated in the binary, but the existence of these classifications, this splitting of experience into black and white is ubiquitous. Harriet is feeling the intensity of the sad feelings. That makes absolute sense. So do the feelings of helplessness which we, as a culture, have difficulty accepting.

I am raising issues of categorisation and complexity not in relation to her feelings but in relation to her defences shielding other feelings. Defences try to protect one, but in doing so they throw up other feelings which are powerful deterrents against engaging with more fundamental feelings – in her case, tolerating her sense of helplessness.

From the psychoanalyst's perspective the splitting categorising mechanism can also be thought of as developmental. Developing minds feel safer with bad things stored outside of themselves – projected on to malevolent characters such as those we encounter in fairy tales. And as children order their world, the allowed, the not allowed and the attribution of difference form a mental picture of how the world is. It is a way of ordering the world and a way of trying to control it.

Gradually, the child begins to recognise that other minds exist and they think and feel differently – not worse than, not better than, just differently. This development is both troublesome and exciting to the child as she or he begins to navigate opinions and desires that are personal and idiosyncratic. If all goes well, the child's expression of her or his opinions and desires will be welcomed and a confidence will emerge that underpins the sense of being both attached to others while having a sense of one's own being.

This separated-attachment idea depends on being sufficiently securely attached in the first instance. If that has not occurred, if those who raise us have not had us in mind as a separate person who is simultaneously vulnerable and dependent, then the sense of self that develops may feel insecure. A search for certainties will ensue as well as a form of thinking that is caught up in good and bad, in and out, them and us, and so on until new relationships in therapy, friendship or love relationships provide for what attachment researchers and therapists called 'earned security'.

Psychoanalysis and psychological theories of development see the capacity to hold complexity in mind – which is to say, when thinking is not arranged in banishing binaries – as a hallmark of psychological selfhood.

This is not to say that right and wrong are not useful categories but they are not uniformly useful categories. They pertain to certain situations – ethics, morality and so on – but in the realms of emotions, and often in politics, over-simplification is a detriment. It diminishes our capacity to hear another. It dilutes the richness of our inner life and opinions. It weakens our resilience and it flattens public discourse.

Complexity is essential to thought. There is rarely one story, one subjectivity, one way to look at and evaluate things.

A psychoanalyst is always thinking about the backstory of the person sitting with them. So before we leave Harriet I would be asking myself: what were the family in Zimbabwe responding to when they made the decision for Harriet, her siblings and her mother to leave? What were the political, social and psychological conditions which came to make that decision? Beyond that, how did the consequences of emigration and immigration and the loss of family play psychologically for Harriet's mother and father and grandparents? How did Harriet's mother cope with her disrupted life, and what did she convey to Harriet about loss? Was it unspeakable, disastrous? How did her mother deal with being transplanted to a new country? Did Harriet experience her first double loss when she arrived in the UK bereft of her father and wider family and with a mother who too would have been bewildered and possible preoccupied as she made a new life. And how did the smaller family unit find pleasures, and were they acknowledged?

I'm spelling this out because complexity and category-making are the dialectical prerequisites of being human. We all struggle with the tension between the two poles of questioning and certainty. Out of that tension comes enormous creativity.

Helen

First Session

Helen is in her late twenties. She has been coming to see me for eighteen months. She's very much a privileged middle-class Londoner, hyper-cosmopolitan, well travelled and, along with her contemporaries, sees herself working in New York, Hong Kong or Sydney for a time. She was successful at school and university and has landed a job in a prestigious law firm. She's tall, with blonde hair, long fingers and an inviting smile. Outwardly, she's extremely confident, but inside, troublingly insecure. She's planning to marry Rob, her boyfriend of more than four years. He's a heart surgeon, warm and supportive, and comes from a similar background. Of late she has been interested in discovering a bit more about her inner life and what makes her tick, but she's skittish and sticking with an idea or feeling isn't easy.

Helen   How are you?

Susie   OK thanks.

Helen   I had a bit of an, um, just a bit of a weird weekend really.

I just did, um, something just, ah, yeah …

Um, I was at this thing and I ended up, ahh, um, I don't really know how to, sorry, I'm …

[*Long pause*]

Helen is in danger of stalling, and I sense she needs a question to get some words out.

Susie   Where were you? What was it?

Helen   It was just a work thing but I just … Oh … I just, like, slept with this man.

Susie	Uh-huh.
Helen	Emotionally and morally it's not OK, but physically it's just someone's skin on your skin, you know.

She looks at me as though she is half wanting me to agree with her, half not.

Susie	Who was this guy?
Helen	He is just a partner in a different firm that I know – it just, this thing, he just was sort of looking at me and … And he was saying some stuff and I just did it … I just did it. In a moment I just did it. I don't know why … I don't really know.

I'm aware of pace here. Helen is taking a while to tell me what she wants to say, but as soon as she has, she is almost racing along describing to herself what she's done.

Susie	Would you want to discover why?
Helen	Yeah, I guess, but …
Susie	How old?
Helen	I guess fifties.
Susie	Uh-huh.
Helen	It makes me feel very sick thinking about the actual bit, 'it', but I think weirder because of Rob. It is just not like me, I don't do that kind of thing, you know, like I just, I have never done that, and yeah, I am just not that kind of person really.

I'm really interested in Helen's use of language. She says 'this thing', 'it', 'I don't really do this kind of thing'. I am holding this speech pattern in my mind as I try to understand what it is that has happened in this encounter.

Susie	So you have surprised yourself.
Helen	Yeah.
Susie	In an uncomfortable way.
Helen	Yeah.
Susie	And were you uncomfortable with Rob last night?
Helen	Yeah in my head, yeah, but not outwardly.
Susie	Yes, we know that is your tendency, isn't it? You are incredibly skilled at being …
Helen	I know.
Susie	Apparently available to everybody or …
Helen	I know, I know.
Susie	Thinking things – conveying that things are just fine.
Helen	Umm.
Susie	When actually, you have things inside of you that are disturbing and now it's …
Helen	[Crying] Sorry … [Crying … long pause]
Susie	What's going through my mind …
Helen	Yeah.
Susie	… is that you have been trying to bring more of yourself to yourself.

When I say she is trying to bring more of herself to herself, I'm referring to those cut-off parts of Helen that she doesn't really know much about. Her psychological energy was harnessed to achieve from early on. She went to a private girls' school in London, and after a gap year travelling through Thailand, Australia and New Zealand. She read Law at Cambridge. She was then recruited to a Golden Circle law firm. The backstory is that Helen's mother was well-off and middle-class. She did not develop a career outside the family. She was stopped from doing so by her own mother's disapproval and a lack of encouragement from her husband, a successful lawyer.

Helen is the eldest of four and was designated to carry her mother's unfulfilled ambition. In doing so, and doing so well, she didn't discover her own desires or her own ambition. She's arrived where she's meant to be, but there's an emptiness and a sense of purposelessness. The attributes she has developed don't feel integral to her – more as though they are stick-ons.

In the therapy we are tentatively addressing the rather undeveloped aspects of her.

Helen   Yeah, but I don't know who that is. I don't know that I know who I am.

There's a plea in her voice, a hopeless cry almost of not knowing the territory of who she is. It's not anything as crude as being a good girl, although there is that, but it is a sense of being opaque to herself. I feel her frustration. She wants to feel more alive but a low-level depressive state lies behind her charm and what's depressed is this undeveloped and unknown part of her.

Susie   I know, and so maybe this is what this episode is about. It's a blip. It stands in contrast to your competence in everything and being perfect and just lovely to Rob, which may have precluded discovering other things. Blips aren't just smudges that need to be rubbed out. They can be useful to you.

You are considering marrying him, maybe you want to show him a bit of your confusions and your …

Helen   I just – just the thought of, like, expressing that to him is just really – I don't know, just the idea of actually having, like, I don't know, talking about this stuff.

Susie   A conversation?

Helen   Um, um. It would just be weird. [*Laughs*] A conversation, yep.

Susie   One that starts: Oh, I don't feel so good, I'm a bit confused.

Helen   I know, but he would just say, why? I don't think he would understand.

Susie   So then you might find the words to answer his 'why?' just as you have found them here.

Helen   What? I feel weird that I have slept with this man.

Susie   I don't think that's the issue is it? The issue is …

Helen   Well, it feels …

Susie   … that this has cracked something for you, something that you've shown me but you haven't ever taken to Rob. It's the carapace you have which has served you pretty well but it is also …

Helen   It is just, like, he's really nice, there's nothing …

Susie   Yeah, but it's deprived you. You've felt 'I can't really show who I am, the other aspects'.

Helen   Which ones?

Susie	The muddled bits, the not-so-sure, the one who isn't always striving.
Helen	Yeah, I sort of feel like, I don't know, like I don't know about those things, I feel sort of more – feel a lot …

Reading the words, it sounds like I'm missing Helen. I'm on one track and she is on another. Helen is very interested in concrete thinking, in truths, in facts, but right now something else needs to emerge for her.

I have the impression that I am crowding her out by trying to extend the conversation while being pushed into very concrete thinking. 'Do I tell, don't I tell, he's nice'.

I would like Helen to be able to catch the stray thoughts, the uncomfortable feelings, the things that don't fit, the texture of life that is banished, is sequestered off, is excluded during the day but which causes her anxiety or rebounds upon her in the morning as she is getting up to go to work.

Helen	Yeah, I sort of feel like, I feel fine. What is that look?
Susie	It was a look with a question mark.
Helen	[*Laughs*] I feel fine, I just feel fine.
	[*Long pause*]
Susie	Do you think this has got anything analogous to when you feel you need to cut yourself, to wipe out something that's difficult and that what you are doing here is actually trying to bring it here rather than banish it.

Helen's been periodically cutting her arms. She started during her A-levels. It has usually been provoked by a difficult feeling or a feeling which overwhelms her that she doesn't know what to do with. The cutting has historically provided some relief. It allows her to sob and wash away her confusions. A growing discovery for Helen in the therapy is that feelings can trickle in without having to be suppressed. There isn't just an on or an off tap. Most of the time, as we see, she still likes to square things away, and when she can't, she can become distraught.

Helen   I suppose I feel sort of quite, like, lonely a lot of the time.

Susie   Uh-huh.

Helen   But that doesn't make any sense because I am surrounded by people all the time.

Susie   Well, alone isn't the same as lonely.

[*She looks at me quizzically*]

You could be missing some bits of yourself.

This 'lonely' that Helen is now touching on is a crucial piece of her difficulties. It relates to the focus on achieving. Taking exams, getting into the prestigious school and university and law firm and finding a boyfriend with a similar family background have driven her. They link her to others, but it is a lonely linkage as she is only present as a surface.

Living, knowing herself, is a foreign idea. She's intrigued but a bit bemused by the idea that she is lonely.

Helen   But what bits? What am I lonely for? What am I missing?

Susie   The way you have described it to me it seems like, instead of these bits of you being tucked inside of you, they are off somewhere else almost outside of yourself. And when they emerge, they kind of boomerang back on you and you find them disconcerting.

> I think what we have been trying to do is help you get
> to know those aspects, and I suppose the weekend was
> an explosion of something that seems so alien that it is
> usually kept outside of your awareness.

As long as Helen is surrounded by people and tasks and knows what is expected of her, she can function at a very high level. On her own, she isn't really sure of who she is. She feels empty and lost. For her, it's a blessing that she has to work long hours and go along with the mantra of work hard, play hard.

Helen   Yeah. I sometimes feel though, like, what is the actual point, like what is the point?

Susie   Uh-huh.

Helen   What is it actually for? Like, why am I getting that person more money and not this person? What am I doing? Am I going to be there at that same place or some other just the same, doing the same things for my whole life?

Susie   Good questions.

Helen   Well, then what? So I just get, like – go and work in a surf shop or something. [*Laughing*]

Susie   [*Laughing*] I think this is a really good illustration of your thinking process, which goes something like: if I'm critical or uneasy at my high-prestige law firm, then there's nothing.

Could I ask you to maybe take a pause and see if there are bits that have meaning for you as well as the bits that are difficult, that might be more nourishing?

Helen   Is that the point?

Helen has got a rather black-and-white reality, so if she is not the successful lawyer and that doesn't make sense to her any more, then she might as well do something designated by her education and social class as useless – to go and work in a shop, as though there is nothing that has meaning. I am trying to slow her up here, to see if she can conceive of herself as having meaning wherever she might be.

At another level she is asking about the meaning of life – an existential question we can all find ourselves reflecting on from time to time – but which for her has an urgency given that she has, without realising it, been following the lead of others rather than discovering her own.

Helen   Is that the point?

Susie   Well it isn't *the* point; there are many points.

Helen   What is *the* point?

I was just sitting on the tube on the way in this morning, I was just like, right, so this is it, you know, this is the – I have been on this tube forever and I'm going to stay on this tube forever.

But don't you feel it as well? ... [*Pause*]

At all? ... [*Pause*]

Susie   It is very hard to be missing a lot of yourself and your experience.

Helen   Yeah but that is so abstract, isn't it? Like what does that actually mean, that you can say that?

Susie   Well, I think what it means is that when you wake up in the morning and you have all of that anxiety, we could try to slow it down and see what it is there for.

Helen   Right – [*visibly relieved, she sits up attentive*] – OK, yeah, oh right, so it, it's as if it's trying to tell me something is it?

Susie   Yeah, it's both shielding you, but it's also – it's a signal, it's
              a 'giving you something'.

Helen   Yeah definitely, definitely.

Susie   So maybe we could just consider it without it driving
              you to take an action. I think when you feel uneasy, you
              rocket into action. Action has given you a certain comfort,
              but there isn't always an easy resolution or an emotional
              solution to what's troubling you. Action makes you feel less
              feeble because you feel yourself to be doing something –
              but sometimes we need to put action to one side …

Helen   Um, um, um, um …

Susie   To consider privately and slowly what the signal is. Some
              space might then open up. And in that space questions
              like 'Do I want to be a lawyer?', 'Do I want to be X?', 'What
              am I feeling now?' might emerge, and if you don't shut
              them right down, by actions or attempted solutions, such
              reflections might lead you to what you are missing that is
              producing this sense of loneliness.

Helen   OK. Yes. Yes. That makes a lot of sense … I feel less jangled.
              Yes … Thank you.

Susie   See you on Tuesday.

Helen   OK Susie, thanks.

Helen has never found the 'I' in herself. She has followed the path
of doing well and it has left her bereft of herself. Now I am suggesting that her internal psychic furniture can be rearranged and there
might be quite a few interesting pieces in there that she might be
able to sit on, lie on, or enjoy.

I chose not to take up the issues around sexuality or being desired
and desiring that sleeping with this older man might suggest. Nor

did I pursue with Helen the meaning of the man's age. It's not that I think these issues are insignificant, but therapy always involves judging what is most salient at a given time. I do know from Helen's history that her father – a man now in his late fifties – was quite remote and, from her perspective, controlling. He was a commercial lawyer, and Helen has wondered why she has chosen that same branch of law to practise in. He had admired her diligence and taken pride in her prizes at school, but he wasn't much interested in recognising her work ambitions. She has longed for his approval for her work success.

She'd been pleased by attention from senior partners – both male and female – at the law firm. When she's described a male partner's approval, she has felt a frisson as though she were entering into forbidden territory. It would be easy to interpret this as essentially sexual. I am not convinced that it is. Nevertheless, it does seem to me to have something transgressive about it. The transgression could be to do with her daring to resituate herself and the possibilities that she has now opened up for herself. This contests the view her father had of her. He saw her as delightful but not serious and certainly not someone who should have serious work ambitions.

While she can do the job that she has easily enough, her being seduced by a 'father figure' at another law firm might be Helen's way of getting some undergirding for her ambition from a man similar in age to her father. Her father may not be prepared or able to give this recognition, so she has unconsciously sought it herself, but in doing so she's felt that she's punished herself because the act of sleeping with this man has compromised her morality.

The reader may be wondering, is this a classical Oedipal situation? The daughter sleeps with a proxy father? I don't think that is a particularly useful interpretation. The motivation may well be to find support and approval from an older man at work and to unconsciously 'show' her mother that she can be a professional woman and sexual, but I am not sure how such an interpretation at this point would help Helen with her struggle to feel authentic in herself.

Second Session

It is eight months later, and Helen, still working as a lawyer, and still with Rob, has recently had an early diagnosis of cancer, which has been treated. Her skittishness has been modified, and she is full of questions about her work and her relationship.

Helen   Susie, hello.

Susie   Hello.

Helen   How are you?

Susie   Fine, thank you ... and you?

Helen   Good actually, yeah, I'm good. Yeah, I feel different somehow today, yeah.

Susie   What kind of different?

Helen   I love it when you look at me like that.

I think she means with interest annd curiosity.

Helen   It's strange, when we got the all-clear last week, it's what I knew and it's what I hoped for and what they suspected would happen anyway because it was so early, but you can't forget something like that. It's still there – I mean it could come back at any point – and I never thought I would be one of those people, you know, I never thought it would be me.

Susie   Yes.

Helen   I suppose you never do, it's just you hear about it so much and then when it actually happens, and the idea that if I hadn't gone in so early, and if I hadn't seen that sticker on that wall of the gym, you know, I wouldn't, you know, and my friend's sister having died last year so quickly from being undiagnosed, it's just, it's just … it's just a bit mind-blowing, isn't it? Then I started to think that there was a reason for me noticing that sticker. Suddenly my attention came to it, it's that CoppaFeel, that charity that great girl has set up from being stage four and wanting to actually do something. She is only twenty-three – it's like, why had I not noticed that before? And if my perception is more acute or something, it is beyond me, in a sense, that is there something, something I didn't know was going on?

Susie   It's an interesting question. We don't know, because we can't reconstruct this, whether you actually felt your breasts, didn't realise you were feeling your breasts, felt something that you didn't …

Helen   Yeah, subconsciously.

Susie   You didn't like, or was a bit different.

Helen   Yes.

Susie   And then noticed the poster.

Helen   Do you think, yeah, do you think I am being silly then thinking …?

Susie   I think you are feeling very relieved.

Helen   Yeah.

Susie   And sometimes when we are relieved we seek explanations for …

Helen   Ah, really. God, maybe I am more … I know that the weirdest thing is that it's made me feel more present.

Susie   Yeah, I think that is the other paradox. Because you are sorting what matters and what doesn't matter, and you're feeling everything so much more vividly.

Helen   Yeah, it's funny. Before, the days kind of stretched
          before me, and now since the day I got the diagnosis
          and I walked out – I said this to you before – it felt like I
          am seeing things in high definition suddenly; what if I
          wasn't here tomorrow, and I thought this wasn't here, but
          actually it's me, you know, and therefore what is me? Is
          this the me that I am supposed to be living as?

Susie   It is quite a moving thought really, isn't it?

Helen   Yeah.

Susie   Because you'd been on a search.

Helen   Yes, I know.

Susie   For you, and then there was all of a sudden a clock that
          said ...

Helen   But that's why I think it's funny that, yeah, I suppose that's
          why I'm questioning whether it was coincidence or what
          it was, you know, because it's making me question a lot
          of things, even going back to work and what I spend my
          hours doing. Kris Hallenga, I think her name is, started that
          charity, and it makes me think, am I really meant to be
          sorting out people's contracts?

Susie   Well, that was a question from before, wasn't it?

Helen   I know.

Susie   And maybe it is quite safe that you have got somewhere
          to go to work and they've been accommodating, but it is
          an opportunity to see if this is the bit of law you do want
          to be doing, or indeed do you want to be doing law.

Helen   And you know what, getting the all-clear is like there is
          something weirdly – I mean, yes, like you said, it's a relief,
          but it's also this ... that is hard, to say. I felt, you know,

anxiety, and this is because you helped me identify it. I might be wrong, but I think the anxiety came out of a sense that I don't want to lose this moment.

Susie   You mean you don't want to slot right back into everything as it was.

Helen   Yeah, yeah.

Susie   Yeah.

Helen   You know …

Susie   I think that is very understandable that you want to take this opportunity.

Helen   Yes, and …

Susie   The opportunity that's your life, that is you.

Helen   Yeah, I read something about the musician Wilko Johnson. He was terminal and he's still here. He described it as he feels like now he's parachuting back to the land of the living, and actually there's something slightly comatose about that land. That really resonated with me because it made me feel like I don't want to be asleep, you know, and I know we've talked about the fact that, you know that thing that happened last year with Rob and me deciding just to get on with it, I wonder whether it was me trying to leave myself and the situation in which I was you know, treading on day after day, without questioning.

Susie   I think you've got a real conundrum, haven't you, because you want to stay alive to this 3D or high-definition.

Helen   Yeah, I know, and I feel, like, anxious with it.

Susie   The intensity of it is exciting, but it's challenging.

Helen   Do you know what it reminds me of, Susie, it reminds me of when I first fell in love with Rob.

Susie   Aha.

Helen   Five years ago, and then everything became high-
                definition, and then it wears off, you know. I don't know if
                that's me, I don't know if that's what chemically happens
                or whether you stop seeing the truth and actually what
                you then see is – or you, yeah, you stop looking and … I
                mean, this week I have been at a couple of appointments
                and Rob missed the second one, and it's not that I
                expected him or needed him to be there, but I felt his
                absence in a more emotional sense, you know. He had
                this work thing or whatever, and then he got home and
                he was sort of detached, and it is not that I want him to
                invest in – you know, I understand that, I'm dealing with
                this myself and it's my thing, I don't want to transfer too
                much onto him, I know we've talked about that, but I, we,
                were sitting on the sofa and I was just looking at him and
                thinking, 'Is that it?' and …

Susie   Were you able to say how you felt?

Helen   No.

Susie   Sorry to come back with the kind of question that I'm
                always asking.

Helen   I know.

Susie   Well, could you say it to yourself, even if you couldn't say
                it to him? You've said it's OK to deal with this on your own,
                but how did you feel about having to go to the second
                appointment alone?

Helen   Two things – I felt weirdly fine and I felt weirdly angry.

Susie   Uh-huh.

Helen   You know, I can identify it as anger, but it didn't come up
                as anger, it came up as numbness, and that's kind of the

	thing that I don't want, that's the old me. I felt like I expect him to be there because he's there, not because I actually want to share it with him necessarily.
Susie	Uh-huh.
Helen	Do you know, and that's scary, and then maybe I'm sitting looking at him thinking … maybe it's an attacking thing, but I don't know if, I don't know what my feelings are for him.
Susie	What's the attacking thing that you stopped before you said, so I couldn't quite get it?
Helen	Oh, I don't know, it's hard to know whether I'm – it's an attacking impulse to try and distance, or whether it's actually a bad thing to have thought, you know, maybe I want more than a marriage and kids with him.
	And that's really scary because it's like, I don't know, I don't know because I love him but do I, is he …
Susie	Well, I think the question is an important one to consider from your side. I also think – and this is a bit of a refrain – but more urgent now, that you haven't talked together. He might not be able to handle what's happened, he might be so scared of losing you.

Helen seems not to have been able to countenance the idea that Rob may have had his own response to her diagnosis. She's been drawn to him as a rock, but in that designation there is also an inadvertent ignoring of what might have been going on for him. He's a doctor, in the business of saving lives, and yet, as we know from protocols, doctors don't treat their loved ones because of their own emotional attachments, which may not be obvious or a hindrance but might just get in the way. That doesn't mean, of course, that we know what his feelings might be regarding Helen's diagnosis.

Helen   Do you think? He just feels like he's not there.

Susie   That he cuts off? Has he got sufficient capacity to share what he is experiencing? And then you're not feeling undergirded, and neither perhaps is he.

Helen   Yeah, I feel like, I don't know if …

Susie   He's your person to be with in this, to be going through a difficult time in your life.

Helen   Yeah, yeah. But it is also, what version of myself am I with him? What version of myself am I?

Susie   And what happens if you're the high-definition version?

Helen's wondering about what version of herself she is, or wants to show us. We still have work to do in enabling her to integrate the different states of being that make up who Helen is. She has allowed herself to be vulnerable and curious about the different aspects of herself that are emerging, and I'm intrigued at her description of 'what version' of herself she is.

Helen   Yeah.

Susie   What happens?

Helen   Yeah, I know, 'cos you know I'm thinking, if I hadn't got it early, and it could come back tomorrow in a different form, and if that's the case, I don't want to go back to sleep. I just wonder whether Rob is tied up with that. Maybe it's irrational, maybe it's just because, at the same time I'm anxious to lose that feeling because we had a conversation last year and he said I want two kids because it would be better for a car if we have to take stuff in it, you know. And that …

Susie   So you're into finding the banal at the moment in him, and that's disappointing for you. Look, there's him, there's you, and then there's the relationship. There is the relationship you've created together, which may not serve either of you as richly as you would like it to be, and it may be able to open up or it may not. It makes sense to be exploring this now.

Helen   Yeah, it's terrifying because it's like, without that, what am I and without him …

Susie   Well, isn't the question who are you? Not what am I?

Helen   Yeah, but I thought I was him. It's a feeling that's very in my body, you know.

Susie   Say more.

Helen   It's like a – I can't get rid of it, I can forget for a minute, then it comes back. It's a sort of, it's hard to explain, it's like a sort of internal itch.

Susie   What are you flicking away there?

Helen   Just, it's in … it's like something inside, I don't know how to explain it Susie.

Susie   Right. I might have lost you and I don't want to. You said I think I was …

Helen   It's like something I need, that, there's something, it's like my veins are itching.

Susie   Because they're inflamed?

Helen   Maybe. But it's like I can't express whatever it is.

Susie   Your veins are the things that carry your blood.

Helen   Umm.

Susie   And they go all through your body.

Helen	Umm.
Susie	And they're – the fact that you are aware of them …
Helen	Yeah.
Susie	You know what it's reminding me of?
Helen	Umm.
Susie	And maybe this is a hell of a jump, but it is reminding me of when you used to have to cut to see that you were alive.
Helen	I know, yeah.
Susie	And I'm wondering what the message is in the itchy thing.
Helen	I know, what is the message?
Susie	It might be something that you've designated, not as a present but as wanted – desire perhaps – longing.
Helen	What if – see, we have a wedding next weekend and I'm dreading it.
Susie	Say more.
Helen	I'm just dreading the same old same old. He gets on that suit he wears, you know, I go buy something new, we get in the car, it's just me and him, ah …
Susie	Is it because you are imagining it being your wedding and that's what the dread is?
Helen	I don't know.
Susie	Or is it you're just in a circle where that's the age you all are and …
Helen	No, it's more the car journey, [*laughing*] why do you look like that?

Susie	I'm asking, what's in there, or what doesn't happen in the car. The look is, I suppose, I'm surprised and interested.
Helen	Yeah, but then I don't know what the alternative is … what is it supposed to be like?
Susie	Well, supposing you were telling him who you are now.
Helen	Right, yeah, I don't know, I can't imagine that.
Susie	Well, you manage to say it here.
Helen	I think he'd just say, don't be silly, it's fine.
Susie	What, if you said, I'm living life, I'm feeling things in a very intense way and it's making me question everything about …
Helen	Oh, I can't imagine having that conversation. Isn't that weird?
Susie	Well, the reason I think it is particularly weird is that you drew a comparison to it when you first fell for each other, and I presume you brought some of yourself to that, and you told him who you were and you found out who he was. The car journey could be a very good opportunity …
Helen	To talk?
Susie	Yes.
Helen	I don't, yeah. What am I scared of?
Susie	You are scared of finding out presumably that he's not the right person. You are scared of finding out that your relationship *is* right and it's got to go deeper. Anything in between those two bands.
Helen	Umm.
Susie	You are scared of being open perhaps in a way that makes the things not fit in the car with the two children and enough room for all the gear.

Helen   Oh, it's such a sickie feeling you know. Yeah, it's just, it makes me feel sick.

Susie   What, the effort of bringing yourself to him?

Helen   Yeah, and saying I don't feel … I'm feeling something but I don't feel the same.

Susie   Is there a way to provoke the conversation where, instead of feeling you're boxed in, you could talk about how this has been a hell of a thing we have both had to go through?

Helen   Yeah, we've never had that conversation, I know. I don't think he knows how to deal with it – he doesn't, he isn't, he can talk about the practicalities but it's very practical. I mean that's why I'm searching for maybe something greater in the sense of 'Is this what it is?' It's blood tests and then you go back to the usual, you take the pill every day and you just go back to work and pretend that it never happened.

Susie   Well, you've been so active in your own treatment and thoughts.

Helen   Yeah, I know.

Susie   And I'm wondering whether you could apply that activity to finding out how he's feeling and how he's been, and whether that would then open up a way for you to have a conversation.

Helen   Um.

Susie   In which you also could say what it's been like for you, as opposed to everything is so neat and tidy and appointments and everything, I think there is something that you're edging towards.

Helen   So what do I, how do I, what do you, how do I start that, Susie?

Susie   Well, at the wedding, you've got an hour and a half in the car. It's a beginning …

Helen   Yes.

Susie   Wouldn't it be helpful to know how this whole period has affected him?

Helen   Yes, that's true.

Susie   And that's a place to start.

Helen   That's true. But you know what? Maybe I feel angry that he doesn't express that.

Susie   Yeah, but maybe that's the point of being a couple. Maybe one person can't do it without a prompt and without the …

Helen   Do you know what else came up? The other day he tried to have sex, and I said I wasn't feeling well but I was, and I was relieved that I had an excuse and that is …

Susie   OK, so I think that you're just confirming what we're saying, because if that is his way of getting close and it wasn't what you wanted …

Helen   Well, I know, but it's been ages anyway.

Susie   And you didn't want it at that time because you're not feeling close. You need to find a way to see whether there *is* closeness, and language might be another way of doing and feeling this.

Helen   Och, yuck. Then you know, maybe you're right Susie, maybe I need to have this conversation, but you know what's terrifying is that if I hadn't had cancer, maybe this conversation wouldn't be happening now.

Susie   Maybe not as urgently, but I think we've had some hints.

Helen   Umm, have you, really?

Susie   Yeah, I think the incident with the partner in the other firm was a hint that you needed or you were feeling distant or something was changing inside of you and you wanted to connect differently to Rob, and now this has given you an opportunity.

Helen   Yes.

Susie   Adversity has given you the impetus, and it will be useful to see whether you can imagine that you can actually get beyond that ugh clutched up feeling.

Helen   Yes, because it is interesting that when the diagnosis happened I felt closer to him instantly for about a week, and then the distance came back, so it is hard to identify whether it's me or it's him.

Susie   Or both of you.

Helen   Um.

Susie   Couples are really good at adjusting to each other, and when things open up, there are possibilities for both of you in a relationship; when things close down, there's a very small area you can operate in.

Helen   What's the point of staying in something?

Susie   You tell me.

Helen   Because it's there, because the unknown is unknown.

Susie   Well, there's not much point in going somewhere else if you're not going to take yourself with you, so you might as well experiment here.

Helen   Well, what if I already have, what if I'm meant to experiment somewhere else, can you only find that out by experimenting here?

Susie	No, I don't think there's one way to do things, but I'm not sure, you know, I think this is …
Helen	Is the other side scary or scarier than this side, or is that a fantasy, either way scared, better or worse?
Susie	I don't think we can be prescriptive but I don't see why …
Helen	Why.
Susie	Avoiding … you have a long history with him, why isn't it worth trying to see if there's some more depth.
Helen	I think I'm angry.
Susie	Yeah, I think maybe you are, but I think maybe behind that anger is either a disappointment or a complacency or your engagement in it, and there's a lot to say.
Helen	Saying something is more terrifying than not, though, or more uncomfortable, but then I suppose that's the whole point isn't it, yeah.
Susie	Uh-huh.
Helen	Oh no, Susie! Going to have to do it.
Susie	Well, look, you haven't got to do it this week, we're meeting again, but would you ponder on that?
Helen	OK, yeah, I will. Why do I feel annoyed?
Susie	You're probably annoyed with me that I've heard what you're saying.
Helen	That's funny, yeah, I'm livid. Why is that a paradox?
Susie	Well, maybe you think you can just come and dump things here, but actually we're interested in you, so I'm not just a rubbish bin.
Helen	No, do you feel like that?

Susie   No, that's too strong. What I mean is that this room, our relationship, isn't just a place for you to take the pressure off.

Helen   Yes, I know, of course it isn't, of course it isn't.

Susie   It's about what's bubbling, what's exciting, what's troubling, what's possible, and I think that's where we are.

If therapy is just about letting off steam, then it isn't therapy. It doesn't provoke change; it just keeps things in stasis. Of course sometimes, because it is the only place to speak honestly, it can feel like the individual is depositing their emotional waste, but that is on the way to being able to explore, understand and assimilate conflicts.

Helen   Possible, that's what it is, isn't it?

Susie   Yeah, that's possible.

Helen   That's so scary.

Susie   So on that note …

Helen   OK.

Susie   Yeah.

Helen   Don't look at me like that.

Susie   I'm not going to look at you like that. I'm going to send you home.

Helen   But I'll think about it.

Susie   I don't think you'll be able to not think about it actually, which may be helpful.

Helen   Yeah, OK, helpful, yeah, yeah, that's good. It's all good, isn't it?

Susie	Well, you don't have to make it better for me, I think we just have to accept there's enormous changes going on.
Helen	Oh my God.
Susie	Or challenges – maybe we'll call them challenges.
Helen	Challenges, OK.

Helen is exploring whether she wants to stay with Rob and can make a life with him. He ticks all the boxes on a social level, and they've enjoyed things together in the past. But the changes in Helen, before the cancer diagnosis and since, have reinforced concerns that they might not make the kind of partnership she wants. She is frustrated with Rob's difficulty with opening up or initiating conversations about his emotional state, and also aware that she herself doesn't know how to broach the kind of conversation she wants. Part of her wants to leave that relationship while part of her is recognising her own difficulties with opening up herself. This is often a challenge: you meet at a point and make a relationship which in itself often provides a spur to emotional growth so that both parties are changed by their relationship. Then life trundles on and ways of being together can settle into quite satisfying patterns, but it can also ossify and the excitement that brought the couple together evaporates, which leads one or other to question its viability.

Therapy has often been accused of creating a wedge in relationships. My experience is quite the opposite, in that I'm aware of looking to see where relationships can – if there is sufficient desire – be strengthened. Of course, damaging, controlling, hurtful relationships which we find out about in therapy need unpicking, and the individuals need help to understand their pull to a difficult and wounding relationship so they are able to leave.

Charles

Charles is in his fifties. He's been coming for five months. He's the co-owner of an advertising agency currently involved in merger talks with a new media company that make him uneasy. He is blond and blue-eyed, extremely good looking and dressed in a bespoke suit with a light-grey linen V-neck T-shirt. His casual elegance is at odds with the storms inside of him.

Charles   Susie, hi, it's Charles.

Susie   Come on in.

Charles   OK.

Susie   Hi Charles.

Charles   Hi, how are you? Can I take my jacket off, it is a hot day.

Susie   Please.

Charles   Well, um, I know you are going to ask me if anything has happened since last week and, yeah, something has really. You know the merger with the …

Susie   Uh-huh, the agency.

Charles   The ad agency, yeah, well I am being pressured from all sides and what I didn't tell you was that – it sounds pathetic, I know – is that I used to be a very heavy smoker. I have not smoked at all for ten years exactly. My father-in-law died of lung cancer really slowly and horribly ten years ago. Caroline and I, because of the children and because of my health and because of her, she begged me to give up, which was hard, but I did it. I did hypnotherapy, eventually, and it took a few months, but I gave up, and I promised Caroline, I promised her that we would be a non-smoking family. And about a month ago I was so frustrated at these young whizz kids that are trying to squeeze us, we are an old-fashioned agency that has integrity …

Susie   Uh-huh.

Charles   That's what we stand for, integrity. We were all, the three
                of us were all at school together. We set it up, our by-line
                is you can't put a price on integrity, and now, for heaven's
                sake, we are being pushed into an area that in my late
                fifties I don't want to go.

Susie   Uh-huh.

Charles   And I started smoking, I don't know why: not heavily at
                first. It was like these three boys who came in, so health-
                conscious and fit and young, and they are taking us over
                and I just wanted to go, screw you, you know. It's like a
                sort of – so I just smoke a couple in a day outside the
                office, and I actually held up a meeting because I said, I'm
                sorry, I am going outside for a cigarette, which they were
                revolted by.

I'm intrigued by the conjunction of the media-company, health-
conscious men who are surprised by Charles's smoking behaviour,
his disdain for them and his wish to show them his contempt for
them. What's the gap he can't bridge here?

Charles   Anyway, it's not something I am particularly proud of.

                Then I started smoking more and what is it today, Friday
                – Monday, Tuesday … Tuesday this week I was in a pub
                in Richmond with my tennis partner, he went out for a
                cigarette so I went into the garden, and I wasn't going to
                have one, then I had one, and Will my oldest walked into
                the garden. He didn't look at me, he saw me but then he
                looked away, then left, he didn't speak. And we have kind
                of been avoiding each other as I caught him smoking
                about eighteen months ago, I suppose, and we came
                down really heavy.

The room chilled as Charles spoke of Will looking away.

Susie   Um.

Charles   Christmas holidays and he wasn't allowed out over
               New Year. He had his money stopped for a month, until
               January. From before Christmas he didn't go out. We
               grounded him, and I made him read stuff about lung
               cancer. He didn't really even know his grandfather, but he
               knew he'd died horribly.

               Roll forward to last week and he sees me. I don't know
               whether he is going to tell Caroline.

Susie   Is that the issue, or is it rather your disappointment with
               yourself?

Charles   That's it. It is an issue with Caroline because we are not
               really speaking at the moment. We are not not getting
               on but we live very different lives. She is in Norfolk for
               four days a week, I get up at weekends and they are jam-
               packed, you know, dinner parties and sailing and tennis,
               so we don't really talk. I know that she would be really
               hurt. And I …

Susie   You know, it really surprises me that in the time we have
               been seeing each other, you haven't told me that she is
               away four days a week.

Charles   I'm not very proud of it.

Susie   Uh-huh.

Charles   We're kind of …

Susie   I suppose that's why you could manage to smoke if she is
               not smelling you.

This is kind of clunky on my part. I'm grappling with several things: his breaking of his promise to himself and Caroline not to smoke, the fact of their quasi separate lives, his dismay about what's happening within his business and his paralysis in relation to his son.

Charles   Exactly. She doesn't – so I don't smoke at weekends. She goes up on a Thursday and she comes back on a Monday. I go up on Friday and come back on Sunday night, so if I want to smoke I can. I know I can stop again because I did, but I just don't want to stop.

Susie   Well, what's in it for you?

Charles   Well I …

Susie   Because there is something significant. It is not nothing.

Charles   No, well, I think it's, it's because it's who I used to be, I suppose. It's linked with the fact that I feel pushed by all sides, you know. Yes, I earn a good salary. If there is a merger, I will still earn a good salary. I have a lot of outgoings – two kids at Marlborough is not cheap, as you know – and two houses and holidays all over. It's like sort of private time for me. Does that make any sense?

Susie   Uh-huh.

Charles   And I've spent a lot of my life disappointing my father, who has no interest in me. I went to Marlborough as well. He went to Marlborough, but he went into a profession: he is in accounting. Advertising in the '80s was not a job to him, you know, and yeah, I've done OK, but even now he doesn't acknowledge it. He's great to Caroline, to the kids, Will and, well, he sent Tom, the younger one, he sent him to camp in America last summer. He never did that for me, several thousand pounds, he can afford it, he's got loads of money, he was an accountant for God's sake, but he just said at Christmas, he just said what do you want? Tom said I want to go to Camp America, so he said fine, I'll pay for it. He never did anything, he never even asked me what I wanted for Christmas.

[*Pause (while Charles feels the hurt and anger)*]

Susie   Can you see his giving to Tom as a way of giving to you?

Charles   No.

Susie   Does it feel like an undercut of you?

Charles   Um.

Susie   Yes. So if we go back to the smoking for a second …

Charles   Yeah.

Susie   If it is a way of giving to yourself or being with yourself, it's pretty thin, isn't it? I mean what is it, eight minutes, a cigarette?

Charles   Not even that.

Susie   How many minutes, and it's furtive.

Charles   Two minutes, you know. I mean, yes of course, I understand there's a nicotine addiction, but that's when you are giving up, that's the hard thing to crack. But yes, I suppose it is thin.

Susie   What is that image of you outside the building smoking?

Charles   I don't know. It is quite sordid, I suppose.

Susie   Is it?

Charles   Well, I suppose it is, but I mean it is what people say: the best people always congregate in the smoking areas, there is a sort of complicity that happens.

Susie   With whom?

Charles   With the other smokers outside, the people that you don't know. Everybody knows that you're not meant to be doing it, and it's not that I am asking to join up to a club, but I don't feel cherished at home, I don't feel cherished at work, I've just really fucked up with Will, and he's basically been out the last couple of days because he obviously doesn't want to confront it with me. I mean, what sort of example is that. Yeah, I know it's bad.

Susie   Well, it's not so terrible if you are taking the time to think about how you are going to talk with him about it. You've found it hard to say that Caroline was away four days a week, and you don't talk with her much and you're not actually talking properly with your partners, so now the need to talk is urgent.

Charles   Uh.

Susie   So this is an opportunity for you to think about the kind of dad you would like to be in relation to acknowledging this difficulty with what Will saw.

It's not the end of the road; it is the beginning of something new and possible.

Charles   Oh right. You see, I didn't hate my dad. I didn't really feel much about him. I don't feel like I have a role model in a way to, you know, I look at, you know other parents and yeah, we've had great holidays. I don't play football, you know. I used to take them to matches and things, but it's not my passion. We play tennis a bit, but I've never been that enviable dad you see in the park who is the rough-and-tumble dad that the kids all absolutely follow like the Pied Piper.

I spent most of my life, I think, wanting my dad to notice me.

Susie	Uh-huh.
Charles	My mum died, so we went away. I went to prep school.
Susie	You know Charles, I know this.
Charles	Sorry.
Susie	No, I'm not saying it for that reason. I'm saying it's as though there is some piece I *don't* know about this, and I don't know what it is, and now I wonder whether it's entwined with the humiliation of being taken over by these three whippersnappers, or whether it's the feeling shamed in front of your son. And I think the reason I stopped you – and I realise it wasn't the easiest thing to hear – is that I think there is an unspoken story of abandonment and loneliness and loss which prevents you feeling you can be present *in the present*.

There's an unfortunate absent presence or present absence that you have reproduced, whether it's with your colleagues, or with your son, or latterly with Caroline, and yet it goes against the way that you have had a family culture, which has really been quite strong. You and Caroline have been quite together in what …

Charles	She's been amazing, I mean she's, she was very young when we first got together and she's – what is she now – forty-six/seven? She has been strong and she's guided, she just let me get on with developing the business and I've never wanted for anything, but I do feel lonely, I feel quite frightened.
Susie	Uh-huh.

Now I'm thinking that Caroline has been doing considerably more of the running of the family relationship than I had realised. Charles relies on her for this, and it has left him unskilled in how to manage

conflicts at work or at home or his feelings about his own father.
Several themes are running into each other.

Charles   You know, I feel much nearer sixty than fifty, and it feels
                 like there is a club that I used to be part of and I'm kind of
                 not.

Susie   Has age come as an explanation for what's missing, so
                 then you go join the bad boys club outside the building?
                 [*Both laugh*] And then get in trouble with your son?

Charles   The unhygienic washing your shirts in the middle of
                 the night because your wife is coming home the next
                 morning. Um, I don't know, yep, I do feel, I can look at
                 myself from the outside.

                 I could read an article about myself as an advertising
                 executive, as a, you know, I could read all that. I could
                 appreciate people's jealousy or amazement or whatever.
                 I don't feel like that, I don't feel like that at all, I don't. I've
                 got friends, you know, not real friends, I've got something
                 that I have created.

                 I don't feel ready to let go of Buchanan's, and yes there are
                 three of us, but *my* name is above the door of the agency,
                 and I, I don't want it to … What's it going to become, Roar,
                 Roar and Buchanan? No, just Roar it will become, with
                 Hoxton trendies, I mean they'll be good, they'll do a good
                 job, they will probably make more money, but you know, I
                 don't feel ready to let go of that.

                 What do you … I mean do you just accept that your time
                 moves on? I don't …

Susie   The piece that is hard for me to get a hold of is how you
                 feel, or how it has happened that the three of you have
                 become a two and a one.

Charles Um.

Susie I haven't quite understood whether you've pulled yourself out of the three partners so that the three of you aren't together, or whether they've been seduced, or were there really sound reasons to merge and because I don't know, and neither do you quite, the accomplishment of what you've created feels like it is just draining away from you rather than being …

Charles Moving to the next stage.

Susie Yah, being appreciated, the reason you are being bought or merging is because you've got something.

Charles Well, we brought in a real whizz kid called Jake, who's now about, he's probably about thirty-eight, and it is through him that we have met this other company, Roar, and he is brilliant, I think he is slightly on some sort of Asperger scale, but he is, he is a genius.

Susie Uh-huh.

Charles I don't particularly like him.

Susie Uh-huh.

Charles You know, I wouldn't want to go out to dinner with him, but you know, he's aggressive and somehow he's managed to get one of the partners to look at a bigger picture, and it just has all galloped.

Susie Yeah, but is your fear of change the thing that has put you on the outside of this rather than …

Charles Yeah.

Susie Allowed you to think wait, would this be interesting? Do I have things to learn? Do I have things to offer?

Charles	Do you know, I hadn't thought of that!
Susie	Uh-huh.
Charles	I've just thought fuck you really, all of you.
Susie	Something being taken away from you.
Charles	Yeah, it's like you know, a favourite toy.
Susie	A big toy.
Charles	Really big toy, I mean.
Susie	Your life.
Charles	Twenty-five years of my life in one business and training before that, and I don't think anybody really appreciates how big it is to me. I don't think Caroline does. Of course, she knows what's going on, but she doesn't, she's not really interested, all she's interested in …
Susie	Well, unless you make it interesting and tell her, it is going to be hard for her to know. Unless you show her what it means to you, not the pounds, shillings and pence, but the …
Charles	I mean I, the alternative is that I just take a back seat and have a nice life, you know, and we travel. We haven't been to Australia. We travel to the places that we've always gone to. We haven't recently talked about things. We used to always when we're holidaying.
Susie	Well, fine, that's maybe what you will do, but until you have got yourself back in the engagement …
Charles	Um, but what is the engagement, what, how would that, how do I do that?
Susie	We have been talking about this for a while.

Charles   Yeah.

Susie   And I am really aware that you actually haven't gone out to lunch and talked with your partners, that it's all around lawyers and negotiations without actually what you created together, or your history together, or what it means, and what's in it for you. I think you've got scared and you removed yourself. I am sure that is not the whole story, but there is some way in which partnership is meant to mean …

Charles   Or you dissolve them, I suppose.

Susie   Yeah, but isn't it worth discovering that first?

Charles   I mean, the complication, well it's not a complication, but, as you know, we were at school together, we're all best men, godparents, you know, that whole sort of mix of, you know, our wives go on holiday together – well, not all of them, two of them do.

Susie   So the smoking's got a lot in it, it's not just got the …

Charles   Two minutes, yeah.

Susie   There's a chance now to think about the challenge and the unravelling, the reconnections, the possibility, rather than the get me out of here.

Charles   Yeah, which, when I'm talking about it, makes … you know, I can see it's pathetic.

Susie   Well, I don't know if it's pathetic but it's, it's such a short-changing of yourself.

Charles   And it can kill you.

Susie   The thing that you are really good at is the creating the story, that's what you do in your job, or did when you were …

Charles   Uh-huh.

Susie   But you haven't been able to give yourself time to have the story about yourself, about what this challenge means to you and asks of you.

Charles   Um, that's harder.

Susie   Harder, yes, that's what you're doing here, but I think maybe instead of a smoke for two minutes, you should come a second time a week.

Charles   Um.

Susie   Or provoke a conversation with your partners and with Caroline, because it is all too compressed.

Charles   But if you compress, then you don't have to think too much in a way. I mean I just, I don't even know what to do about Will. OK, fine, Caroline and I will have it out, you know, at some point there will be … but I don't know, I mean, what, I really care what he thinks about me. I've just been an entire hypocrite.

Susie   No, you've disappointed your son.

Charles   Yeah.

Susie   And you've disappointed yourself, and that's what needs confronting inside of you. How to go about talking or listening to him, or talking with him is in a way another piece which …

Charles   Um, so do you think I should front-foot it, – sorry, I know you're not meant to give me advice in that way, but I don't know how to proceed.

Susie   Well, what alternative do you have? You're not going to be able to hide behind a cigarette.

Charles	For two minutes, twice a day. Um, so I've got to. It's really hard. This may be the way that I was brought up with kind of no communication – it's really – with no communication with my dad, I find it really hard to say sorry to, not just to, to my sons, and yet I love them, I love them most in the world, I don't know what that's about.
Susie	Well, you just said what you thought it was about, is that you don't have a picture of a dad inside of you …
Charles	Yeah.
Susie	That has that capacity, and you're wanting your dad to apologise for not being able to enjoy you and admire your accomplishments and relish what you've done. Moving that package on to what you need to do for your children is not quite accurate. Your children have their own relationship to you. You've been a much more present dad. But dads also disappoint, and I think that disappointment is what is on the table.
Charles	Yeah.
Susie	I think it would be useful to talk about this a bit more, but we have come to the end for today.
Charles	OK, so I'll see you next Friday, yeah.
Susie	OK.
Charles	I can't, I've got a lot to process, just briefly, I can't promise that I'm not going to smoke before next Friday.
Susie	Am I the schoolteacher?
Charles	[*Laughing*] No, but that's … thank you.
Susie	Well, you know, you could use your mouth to speak rather than to inhale.

Charles	Yeah.
Susie	Just a thought.
Charles	Thank you.
Susie	OK, see you next week.
Charles	Yeah, brilliant, enjoy the sun.

Charles came in concerned about his smoking and his son seeing him smoking. The session got diverted into the fact that he doesn't talk much to his wife or his partners, and I left the trouble he feels about talking to his son dangle. For a therapist it is always about making choices about where you go. Sometimes they are unconscious and sometimes quite unbidden. I think my reluctance to talk about Will reflects a sense I got from Charles that he was feeling quite adolescent and didn't yet know how to rise to the occasion.

I have the new information about how unseen he has felt by his dad. He feels unfathered and jealous of what his father can give as a grandfather. He isn't sure how to father, and I feel an urgency to talk about the ways in which he hurts and how the bond he created with his school friends is now fracturing, adding to his rudderlessness. I'm also thinking about his contempt for the young men who want to acquire his company and wondering whether the stance he has taken also encodes his father's (real or perceived) relationship to him, what people might understand as Oedipal rivalry when the son replaces the father being reiterated by the anguish of never feeling he has been accepted by his father.

Charles was sent to boarding school from an early age after his mother died. There is a large literature about the damage of boarding-school culture. Recently our notions of parenting and attachment have meant that harsh separations, emotional and sexual repression and abuse have thankfully to be revised. For Charles, who lost his mother and presumably had little space or support for his grief or the confusing circumstances of leaving home so early, coping meant shutting himself down and learning to manage by not feeling too much. Now, many years on, as his boys are going into the world, his own emotional confusions have returned, offering him a chance to reknit his story not through suppression but through greater self-knowledge.

That knowledge doesn't let me off the hook. It makes me mindful of where we need to go next session, and how to hold on to the threads: Caroline, father, colleagues, Will and smoking.

Richard and Louise

This is Richard and Louise's fourth session. Louise is from Hull, and Richard is first-generation London-born, whose mother came from the Caribbean. He's a compact man, 5 foot 7 inches, with striking dreadlocks, leather jacket and trainers. Louise is the same height. She wears combat boots and a long skirt. Her brown hair is flowy and lush. They are in their early thirties. Louise is about to have a baby, and things have become frayed during the pregnancy.

We can hear the tension in their relationship as they climb the stairs. He's coming as Richard; she reminds him he is coming as part of a couple – Richard AND Louise. The session usually starts with a skirmish.

Louise	Hi.
Richard	Hi Susie.
Susie	Hi, come on in.
Richard	Right.
Louise	Nice to see ya. Um, see, yeah, well we've got to make sure that we leave on time because we are parked in a really dodgy spot.
Richard	It will be alright, it will be alright.
Louise	It probably won't be alright, but as long as we leave on time, then we have got more chance.

Louise is trying to draw me into a conversation about Richard and what she experiences as a certain kind of casualness or neglect, in this instance, about risking a parking fine. He, for his part, is trying to shush her up. This is the pattern they've shown in the previous sessions.

Susie   OK.

Richard   Relax.

Louise   [*Laughs*]

Susie   I'm sorry, I'm not quite getting what's going on between you, or maybe I am!

Richard   No, I just keep telling her to relax, you know, she is just always on at me – things like the car, I just feel like, you know, she's on my case. I am constantly under attack.

Susie   Do you think that you might default to feeling under attack and that in this instance it might be more that Louise is nervous?

Louise   I *am* nervous. I am nervous about money, about time. I think these are the essential problems. I am really aware of the fact that I am eight months pregnant and about to have a baby. In one week's time I will be full term, so the baby could be born then, and yet you haven't been to a nursery shop with me, you haven't bought anything for the baby with me, all your plans are about time out of the house, and it is making me really nervous.

Susie   I think it might help if you, Louise, said 'I feel' instead of 'you do'. That way Richard might be able to hear what's troubling you a little more easily.

Louise   I feel like you are leaving everything to me, I feel quite lonely when I am walking around picking things for our baby.

Richard   Well, you never walk, so I don't know what you are talking about. You never walk, do you?

Louise   [*Laughs*] I never walk!

Richard   You never walk anywhere, you just sit at home all the time.

Louise   That is a ridiculous thing to say. When I go shopping – I don't do it online, I go to a shop and I walk around the shop, that is what I am talking about.

Richard   Yeah, because Mum helps her pick up all the stuff doesn't she, Mum's always there to help you out.

Louise   I am not having a baby with your mother, I am having a baby with you, Rich.

And actually, I don't know which is the better prospect. [*Laughs*]

Richard   Why are you making comments like that? Wh… wh… what is it, what is the thing with my mum? All she wants to do is help out, make sure that you are not lonely while I am out there working hard trying to make sure that we keep the wolf away from the door, and you are ridiculing my mum. What is all that about?

Louise   I am not ridiculing your mum. I'm just saying that I want to make these decisions with *you*, I am having a baby with *you*, not your mum, she is not your substitute and you shouldn't see her that way.

Richard   Alright, alright.

When you are with a couple, they demonstrate how their relationship is and the ways they interact. It can be quite delicate to work out how long to let a dispute run. It might be that their style is to fight and come to a resolution. It might be that fighting creates distance from one another. It might be that fighting heightens their passion. Or it might be that being criticised and feeling beleaguered is a pattern they've imbibed from their parents' relationship or how they were treated. There are so many possibilities when a couple is in the room together that I need to watch it for long enough to know the emotional spaces that each one of them occupies, as well as what they psychologically carry for each other.

Listening to them zigzagging, it is hard for Louise's point – at least, so far – to be heard by Richard. He gets busy pushing her off course by criticising her. In one way it is simple: you're nagging and hassling me so I'm going to get back at you. Inevitably, the more she pushes, the further he backs away or appears obtuse.

Richard appears very laid-back and Louise rather systematic about what's not right and what needs attending to. She's sitting forward intently and he's put himself in the far corner of the sofa, legs spread, quasi-relaxed, quasi-dismissive. Their embodiment mirrors character traits which have psychological significance for them as a couple and each other as individuals. Richard relies on Louise's lists and scolding. He's been responsible from a very early age and very conscientious about earning. He wants to be free of responsibilities that aren't to do with money. Her remonstrations keep him aware of the other things he needs to be doing. She carries his list in her head like an outsourced memory stick.

Louise has always loved Richard's more laid-back attitude. Until the middle of her pregnancy she bathed in it and was able to relax with him. The change has been hard for her as she can't use the laid-back part now for herself. It feels too irresponsible.

Observing how they divide up their psychological ways of being leads to the question of how the therapist can intervene to reshape those places which they once valued in each other but which aren't working now. My job is to help them walk alongside each other, to amplify their voices to each other so that they can hear one another, rather than be alternately bounced on a seesaw of 'you're the baddy', 'no, you're the baddy'.

Susie   We talked last week about how hard it is for you to imagine being a dad. You are giving Louise your mum rather than giving her yourself. Maybe it will be very different when the baby arrives, but I sense that up to now it feels like it is just a scary proposition.

Richard   Yeah, I guess I have been thinking about my dad.

Susie   Uh-huh.

Richard   I mean, yeah, but I am not going to be like him, I mean I'm not going to disappear like he disappeared.

Louise   Richard, you already *are*. You're not around. You haven't been around.

Like, I find it difficult, I find things difficult, I can't even reach my boots to zip them up at the moment 'cos my stomach's in the way. God knows how fat people cope. But you don't help me do these little things.

Susie   So in other words, Louise, the caring that you used to experience and must have been part of the reason you wanted to have a family together, has disappeared. And Richard, you may not be aware that you would spontaneously go towards looking after and looking out for Louise.

Louise   That's exactly it.

Richard   Yeah, maybe.

Louise   It's like ...

Susie   Sshhh, let him think.

I have the sense that Louise's understandable grievances are crowding Richard. She sees it as him running away, but for him to reflect on what she is upset about Louise needs to back off. Otherwise we are in a psychological cha-cha routine where he retreats, she chases or criticises, and he retreats further. This maintains the same distance between them rather than the beginning of a coming together.

Richard	Yeah, I mean the dynamic's changed, it feels like some of the fun, some of the fun's gone, you know, it's – I thought having a kid was meant to be fun, you know, and we're meant to be, you know, celebrating this journey, but the vibes I am picking up all the time just feel passive-aggressive.
Susie	What about your own vibe inside, Richard? Do you think it's possible that you might be quite a bit more scared than you know, than you acknowledge to yourself?

When working with a couple, you can see the projections they foist on each other. He's making the problems all about her, and she's making them all about him. By asking him to listen to his own vibe, I'm hoping to move him from a defensive attacking and rather dismissive position to see what feelings and fears he is dismissing inside himself.

Richard	Oh yeah.
Louise	What are you scared of?
Richard	I guess how I'll mess it up.
Louise	[Laughs]

And as she laughs she herself becomes dismissive of his fears. She doesn't want to know about them any more than he does.

Richard	Well ...
Louise	Yeah, but you haven't even started yet, you haven't even ...
Richard	Yeah, but you know it's like you kinda – you know ...
	Maybe I am more like my dad than I realise maybe. Maybe

the feelings I am having right now are the feelings that he was having. Maybe.

Susie Uh-huh.

Richard You know, these feelings of destruction that I have, you know sometimes I just want to tear the place down.

Louise Oh my God. [*Laughs*]

Richard I do, I just feel like smashing the place up.

Susie Louise, if Richard's telling you what he is feeling, this is so the two of you can connect rather than for you to jump on him.

Richard is showing his fear. This terrifies him. It terrifies Louise, but if both of them can bear it, she will know him better, he will know himself (at this moment) better and it will bring them closer. It will redraw and deepen the emotional field between them.

It sounds like a simple thing to do, but it is a psychological shift for both of them to hear and bear. The fear is a fear he is anxious about. It is not inevitable that he is or will be like his disappearing father. It is not a reality. It is a worry.

Encountering fear doesn't make it bigger or more real. Curiously, it can make it more manageable. Its shape can change and become porous and less monolithic. It's worth engaging with because it will move them into a different and deeper relationship to each other.

Louise for her part will have to expand her view of Richard. She will have to see his vulnerability. If Louise can hear his fears rather than rubbish them, she will add to his capacity to examine and know them. If he can acknowledge his vulnerability, which he is starting to do by expressing himself, he can begin the process of accepting it in himself, aided by her understanding.

Louise	Yeah, but it is pretty frightening to hear that you would want to tear the place down.
Richard	Well, that's how I feel.
Susie	What interests me is that when Richard showed you a bit of his vulnerability, Louise, you kind of pooh-poohed it, pushed it away, or it wasn't good enough.
	You are wanting more closeness, Louise, and part of getting there may be accepting where he is at and where you are at.
Louise	I just feel really far away from him … from, from you.
Richard	Alright, alright, but you know, I'm here, you know. I'm looking out for us, I am not going to run away, am I? The closer we get, I'll get the lads, I'll get the Poles to take over the workload and I will be with you, and Mum will be there as well.
Louise	I don't want your mum there, I'm sorry.
Richard	Why don't you want my mum there?
Louise	Because she is not my mum.
	I don't want your mum at my birth, I don't.
Richard	Why don't you want her at the birth?
Louise	I don't want your mum looking at my vagina, quite frankly.
Richard	What's all that about?
Louise	It's weird.
Richard	Why are you saying things like that, what do you mean, like …
Louise	Well, that's what would be happening.
Richard	She's a woman, you're a woman.

Louise   I don't want to look back and say there were three of us there.

                 I mean I just feel it is such a personal thing and it is something that is potentially so intimate between me and you.

Susie   Right … Richard, is this you again feeling that your mum is sort of a proxy for something you don't know how to do, whereas actually what Louise wants is for you to be there with her? I can understand you are not sure you can do it, but I don't think your mum can do it for her – or for you.

Richard   I'll be there, I'll be there. I'll hold her hand, you know, I'll like – you know, I'll say the things that I need to say.

Louise   Yep, but see you get – look at your body language, you're funny about it.

Richard   What is this?

Louise   Well, you can't even look at me, you've leant forward, you are looking at me like over your shoulder, like I'm an imposter.

                 I am your partner, we made a baby.

Richard   Yeah, yeah, alright, alright.

Louise   I want you to stop putting things in the way between me and you. Not your mum, not your business, not your time away, not your chequebook. I just want it to be me and you. Where have you gone? That's what I want to know.

Richard   Yeah, alright, alright, you're right.

I was wishing that I could shush Louise again so that Richard's words could be heard by both of them and they could clear some ground, but now it is Louise's turn to go zigzagging off … her statement is strong, but timing is all and I wished I could slow it.

Louise   Well, we've come here for therapy and that's really good.

Richard   I'm just not, I'm just …

Louise   He's paying for the therapy, and that's really good.

Richard   You know …

Louise   I see the effort, but where are you?

Richard   That's why we're here right, that's why we're here, because I've made the effort and put the, you know, the things in place that we can come here, so that we can share what's going on.

Louise   But paying for them is not a substitute for intimacy, it's not.

Richard   You talk about money because you know it is always going to be there in some way because I am always going to be providing it, so that is why you have got such a whimsical view of money.

And we are off again … This time it's Richard who can't hear what Louise has said about money being a poor substitute for intimacy.

Louise   Don't talk to me about being whimsical about money.

Susie   OK, so here's what I think. When you get to the thing that needs to be said, one of you goes off.

               So you were saying something, Louise, about how you want Richard to be there, or pointing out he wasn't. He was saying yes, OK. And maybe that yes, OK – his acknowledgement – is the thing that you need to hear, rather than the two of you escalating it. I think it is a scary moment for both of you, and a precious moment for both of you, or a precious time, and I think a little bit more tenderness rather than leaping on each other with how

you are disappointing each other is required, because I
sense you are both very disappointed in each other.

Richard   Yeah ... look I am going to be more engaged, I am going
to be more present, I just need you to be able to see that
sometimes I'm blocked.

Susie   Uh-huh.

Louise   Do you want this baby?

Louise isn't able to hear that sometimes he is 'blocked'. She is impatient with that. She interprets what Richards says as his having gone into a yes-mode, which is dismissive, rather than a being-there mode. He's leaned back again into the corner of the sofa. His words seem pro-forma. I sense he is not deliberately dismissive but feels out of his depth, and troubled.

Richard   Yeah, yeah, of course I want the baby.

Susie   What was that actually? Were you trying to say, Louise, I
have missed you or I am insecure, or ...

Louise   I do feel disappointed and I just feel really upset all the
time ... and I feel rejected before it has even begun, I feel
it is pushing us apart. The more my belly grows it is like a
wall pushing in the way.

I think there is something about her saying a wall pushing in the way that allows Richard to go into a reverie and share what's been troubling him.

Richard   You know, I don't know, it's funny, like the other day I was
looking through my, you know, just some papers, and I
don't know, I came across my birth certificate and it was
a weird moment because, you know, it had my mum's

name on it but it didn't have my dad's name on it. Where it said 'Father' it was just two dashes, you know, and I just thought that was weird, it was kind of, I don't know, it felt like it was a sign.

Louise   A sign of what?

Richard I don't know, I don't know what, I just felt like it was saying something to me, do you know what I mean?

Susie   That there is a void?

Richard Yeah.

Susie   Where your dad was?

Richard Yeah.

Susie   And so you are not sure what you have got to bring to your baby and to Louise, and so you go and work like a madman?

Richard Yeah.

Susie   As a way to do something?

I'm thinking now of how Richard's concerns – albeit largely unconscious up until now – about how present and adequate he can be, have turned into being a provider and working for the soon-to-arrive family. He feels himself to be active in response to the forthcoming arrival, so he feels rather put upon by Louise and her definition that she is doing everything.

Richard Yeah, I guess.

Susie   Uh-huh.

Louise   Baby, you're going to be an amazing dad, you are just going to be amazing, you are. You are nothing like that

> thing, that void, that man, you're not. You don't have to
> be, anyway. Like, that's why we were always going to have
> kids, it was always going to happen, and you were always
> going to be brilliant.

So Louise now has turned her panic and accusation into idealisation, and it is true that Richard is in a different place because he has had a chance to say why he is so frightened. We are ending the session with a sense of two different emotional states going on, two different emotional journeys, extreme intensity and preoccupation on both their parts and the possibility that they might understand what the other is feeling.

What's important for the therapist to convey is that being on the same page with the baby doesn't mean having the same emotional response to this event. Louise isn't going to feel as Richard does. Richard isn't going to feel as Louise does. Being on the same page means each having an ear out for how the other is feeling and each respecting where the other is coming from. In the best of all possible worlds we might be gently suggesting to each member of the couple to become curious about the why of their partner's feelings.

Susie	Alright so ...
Louise	Yeah.
Susie	See you next week.
Louise	OK.
Richard	Yeah, thank you.
Susie	Unless of course ...
Louise	The baby comes.
Richard	Unless of course.

Louise	[*Laughing*] Yeah.
Susie	OK.
Richard	Thank you.
Susie	Alright.
Louise	It's got to wait anyway, we've got to finish decorating the bedroom.
Richard	Yeah, I'll get onto that, don't worry about that.
Louise	Thanks Susie, see you next week.
Richard	See you next week, yeah, thank you.

Becoming a parent is momentous. Moving from being a couple to being a parenting couple is challenging. In this session we have been seeing Richard's concerns expressed as flight. Louise's ways of coping are focused on getting everything ready for the baby and in trying to get Richard to behave more like part of a couple. Her anxiety is an equally potent force, as is her initial incomprehension about his concerns, but in this session the focus has been on helping Richard to recognise his fear.

Both Richard and Louise bring the imprint of their relationships with their own parents to the pregnancy. Richard's mother has been a very available lone parent who has done everything in the household and looked to Richard to be financially responsible at a young age and to help support her. He has managed that since he left school at seventeen. Louise has become the next woman he is looking after financially, although not until the last month.

Louise's mother was quite controlling of her, her sibling and the rest of the family. Her dad was around but disengaged, and Louise's mother would mutter about how neglectful or useless he was. Louise hated her mum's way of being and was drawn to Richard because he was much more laid-back and gave her a lot of space, but as she moves into being a mother, the family constellation is stimulated in her. She sees Richard acting like her father and she has become controlling and full of complaints. She doesn't like it – and we've discussed it – but as her isolation grows, it has become almost a default.

In a couple one sees the trace of the family stories each member emerged from. Often, of course, these are supportive and nourishing. Even so, there may be aspects of their upbringing that they have disliked and have consciously chosen not to reproduce, but when the going gets tough, the difficult bits of the relationships that made them can come to the fore. There is no formula in working with a couple. The endeavour is to give each member the extra beat to hear what the other is saying and wanting while becoming clear enough to express what's on their own mind. That process can illuminate the unconscious entwinements and longings which need addressing. Each couple's story is different and surprises and touches me in unexpected ways. It is the details that I always find enchanting and affecting. Richard's discovery of the two dashes and Louise's bluntness about not wanting his mum in the delivery room. Such details create an empathic curl and warmth in me as I get to know them better.

Ten Months Later

This is their first session since Isaac, their son, arrived. He is now ten months old.

Susie   Hello, lovely to see you both.

Richard   Good to see you again.

Susie   Congratulations.

Richard   Thank you, yeah.

Susie   Come on in.

Richard   Thank you. It always smells so nice in here.

Louise   Yeah it does, yeah.

Richard   Been a while, but yeah. So yeah, I guess we've hit a brick wall, haven't we, really.

Louise   Yeah.

Susie   How so?

Richard   With, it's just this whole modern era, isn't it, of women have a baby and the next thing you know, they want to take a promotion, to be frank.

Richard's tone is mordant and slightly depressed. They go at it full tilt.

Susie   When Louise rang, she told me that she'd gone back to work half-time, with Mum looking after Isaac and now she's been offered a promotion that's making you uneasy.

Richard   Well, already we're not really on the same page. I'm leaving the house at half six, I'm at work all day, I'm fitting the kitchens, it's going well. I've taken on a few more staff and what not, but you know, I come in and I mean you are already not in. Often, Isaac's asleep. I don't really feel like I'm getting a look in, I'm not really involved. You and Mum just chat away like I'm not even there.

Louise   But your involvement is your choice, you have to take responsibility for that.

Richard   Well it's easy for you because you just start breast-feeding every time he starts crying.

Louise   Well, that will change if I go back to work full-time, he'll go on the bottle.

At the moment you've got options, you seem to not want me to have any options. I've got this promotion. It's a chance for me to succeed in both areas, as a mother and as a professional.

Richard   You're going to spread yourself, I think she's going to spread herself thin, I think you're going to spread yourself thin.

I'm wondering whether Richard's concern is for Louise, the baby or himself. It rather feels that his complaint is about their relationship drifting and his losing a grip on what's going on.

Louise   At the moment I have all the responsibility as a parent and you don't have any, and so yes, if I'm the only parent, then I'm spreading myself thin, but if you stepped up it wouldn't matter so much that I was at work.

Richard   I'm keeping us, I'm keeping the ship steady.

Louise   Yeah, well, you wouldn't, you don't have to.

Richard   You say that now, but the work, you never know, next month, you know, who knows what's going on with Europe …

Susie	The first bit of what you said, Richard, sounded like you were missing Louise, and that was happening before the baby came, and now there is something about not feeling included in family life.
Richard	Yeah.
Susie	And you've gone a bit macho about what's to be what.
Richard	Macho?
Susie	Well, you imply she doesn't really earn any money, it's all on your shoulders, whereas it sounds like there is something about neglect or not knowing how to get in there, or missing.
Richard	Maybe, yeah, I mean of course, I mean there's not much affection in the home any more. We don't really, you know, we don't have sex any more. I don't even know the little fella.
Susie	One of the things that I was left with right before Isaac arrived, was you, Richard, feeling very strongly that there was a void …
Richard	Yeah.
Susie	… where a father was.
	You've got a whole life with Isaac.
Louise	Um.
Richard	Yeah.
Susie	And Richard, you are your own boss, and you've got your mum there, and you could conceivably have a few hours with Isaac with your mum, or on your own, or on the weekends so that this doesn't become so mysterious and you don't feel this most major thing that has happened in your life, the thing that you created together, doesn't only belong to Louise, it belongs to both of you.

Richard's complaint about not knowing how to be with his child or partner is occurring because of the way they've arranged things with Louise and his mother being in charge. If one doesn't relate to an infant, it is hard to know how to do so. What appears mysterious becomes less so only by being with an infant.

Richard   Yeah, I mean, I suggest things – let's go and watch the footy on a Sunday. People always take their children to the pub, why can't we take Isaac to the pub, you know? Why can't we do other things, why do we always have to be homebound and stuff? And they don't involve me in any conversations, to be honest, I don't know if it is possible, but can men be, can they be post-natal? I mean, can that happen?

Louise   What do you mean, post-natal?

Richard   Can a man be post-natal?

Susie   Yes I think so, but you have to figure it out in each family.

I missed something here. Richard is flagging up that he's depressed. He's worried about himself. He wants to know if men can get postnatal depression. I've taken it that he doesn't know how to connect with Louise and Isaac and is feeling alone and isolated.

Richard   Right, well, I don't know, there's something going on. I think I need some one-on-one. I thought that you'd understand where I am coming from, I don't know, I think I just need to communicate with somebody that actually has some proper kind of empathy towards me.

I'm a little confused. I don't know whether Richard is talking about one-to-one time with Louise or one-to-one therapy, so I wait to see what unfolds.

Louise   You bat me off before I've even got chance. You've created this wall around yourself. I've got a really special bond with Isaac, but this is purely because I spend 70 per cent of my time with him. The rest of the time I'm at work, and that's only been for the past few months, and I'm just trying to feed myself. If I was to spend every waking hour of the day with him, I would go insane. Going to work has really helped me manage the time that I have with Isaac. If you took some time off work, you know, worked from home a little bit more, took the managerial positon that you have and then just spent a few hours with Isaac … because otherwise what happens is, when Richard is with Isaac, I do, I am aware that I criticise the way he deals with him, but that's because I know the baby a lot better.

The situation is so inflamed that Louise isn't really open to what Richard is frightened of and Richard is critical of Louise and her desires. We've gone into the practicalities as a way to address their disconnection from each other, which makes some sense.

Susie   Yes, Louise, but Richard has to get to know. It is like asking the man to do the washing up and then criticising the way he stacks the dishes, and that doesn't help. What happens on the weekends when you are both around?

Louise   Well, we have promises of doing something together at the weekend, but often Richard's work bleeds into a Saturday.

Susie   Uh-huh.

Richard   It can do, yeah.

Louise   And so then, you know, and the thing is Isaac starts to get tired around sort of mid-afternoon on a Saturday, every

day he just starts to sort of wind down, and so it's not
right, it's not fair to take him to a pub then.

Susie   Why is that?

Louise   When the pubs are really full at the weekend.

Susie   What's the problem with him being asleep in a strappy?

Louise   Well, I just feel that it's not really fair on the baby.

Susie   Uh-huh.

Louise   Um, but if it is just us three at home – Isaac, Richard and
myself – then it very quickly becomes claustrophobic
because we are just not sharing the space very well at all.

Richard   We don't. There's no communication, so we will be in the
room together and she will be in another world, Lou's in
another world, with Isaac. I'll make suggestions, you know,
and you just ignore me.

Louise   But they are completely unrealistic.

Richard   You're more interested in my mum than you are in me.

Louise   Well, your mum's very helpful.

Richard   She used to hate Mum before, she couldn't stand Mum
coming around.

Louise   I didn't hate your mum.

Richard   Now she's her best friend.

Louise   I didn't hate your mum.

Susie   Well, I suppose she's parenting with your mum a bit,
isn't she, and the difficulty is how to create the space for
Richard to get in and for you to relinquish a bit, but be
there so that you can actually have your partnership with
Richard.

What happens when you're in the space together? Can you describe what happens, what it feels like to you, Louise, and why you don't feel you can go to the pub?

Louise   Well, I feel that Richard is exhausted and I'm exhausted.

Susie   Uh-huh.

Louise   But I haven't got the option of just falling asleep on the couch or, you know, having two big glasses of wine or whatever, because I feel that I am the primary carer for our baby, so I feel like I'm having to be the adult all the time. Richard wants my attention, Isaac needs my attention. I feel like I'm parenting two kids, to be honest.

Richard   I just find that incredibly patronising.

Louise   Well, you might do, but that's, that's the bare bones of it.

Richard   I'm not asking you to parent me, I just need to have, you know, a healthy relationship with the mother of my child. Isaac's alright. He's done well, he's got Mum, he's got you, and now you want to bring this alien presence into the home, this whatever, this kind of foreign au pair, into the house, somebody who barely knows our kid so you can swan it around in whatever country your work takes you to.

Louise   Oh, your language, your language …

Richard   Personally I think it's a little narcissistic, to be fair.

Louise   Narcissistic to want to go back to work after ten months of being home?

Richard   I think it is, yeah. I think to be honest there is all this, I don't get all this modern kind of woman thing, but …

Louise   You are just so old-fashioned.

Richard   It's not old-fashioned, it's just like …

Louise   It is old-fashioned.

Richard   Look, my mum, she used to run the home, she was the beacon of that home and there is no shame in that. I don't know why there is a shame in that nowadays, that women feel ashamed to actually nurture a child and …

Louise   I do nurture our child, thank you very much, and I don't feel ashamed of just being a mum but, you know, work's going really well for me at the moment. I was asked if I wanted to interview for this promotion, I didn't go seeking it, and as it happens I've been offered it, it is an incredible opportunity, all I want is the chance to see how it goes, and it is working really well with Isaac and your mum, and then the rest of the time we can have him with an au pair, or a nanny, or nursery, I haven't worked it all out in my head, but why should it all be my responsibility to work out? Why can't you sacrifice your work a little bit?

Richard   Well, I don't mind taking a day here and there, I'm not saying that I'm completely opposed to it.

Louise   Oh, you're not.

Richard   I'm not completely opposed to it.

Louise   Would you do that then? Would you really do that, would you really take a couple of days off work a week, because at the moment you can't even take a Saturday off?

Richard   Work spills over into the weekend, what am I going to do?

Louise   Yeah, well, my work might as well, but I haven't got the option at the moment because you're not there.

              I am supporting you and your professional life.

Richard   Why are you getting aggressive?

Louise   I'm supporting you in your paternal life, I'm getting nothing apart from criticism. I'm sorry, I'm sorry, Susie, but that is how I feel, I feel on fire actually at the moment, I feel incredibly capable.

Richard   I might as well just move out of the house like …

Louise   No, that's not true.

Richard   You might as well do it all.

Louise   No, I wouldn't do that.

Richard   Take a promotion, get a nanny too, I tell you what, while you're at it why don't you put him into public school, private school, put him in there till he's what, fifteen, and then take him out afterwards, see how he's …

Louise   Oh don't be ridiculous, you just get into a strop.

Richard   So, you know, I barely even know what he looks like.

Louise   The reason why I'm patronising, you feel patronised, is because you behave like a teenager. You are making me the adult in this situation. If you offered me something constructive for a change, then that would be a lot better.

Richard   Constructive.

Louise   But you don't.

Richard   I can't win because, you know, if I'm not bringing the money in, if I'm not holding the fort in that respect …

Louise   Bringing the money in.

Richard   I get stick.

Louise   What is this?

Richard   You want me to come home, I've been up since half six, you want me to come in and then you want me to be the belle of the ball and have the conversation and kind of …

Susie	Richard, you said two things: one is you don't have a way into Isaac, and two, you have no idea what is going on with Louise and you don't really get what she wants. The two of you having a slanging match about it is not going to make you find that out. Every new parent has a hard time unless they are from a huge family and they have done a lot of parenting. It is a whole new challenge and some of the questions are: How can you be a dad? What does that mean? And how can you be a partner? Because your mum, who was your mum and dad so to speak, didn't have a partner, and you don't have a picture of more than one person being engaged with a child, you don't have it inside of you.
Louise	Um.
Susie	And I think you're probably very upset that Louise isn't there all the time because you want her there for you.
Louise	Um.
Susie	So you are getting hit from both sides and not knowing how to get in there with her or Isaac.
Richard	Yeah, maybe you're right.
Susie	Could you think about this little fellow and you?
Richard	Yeah, I mean, he's amazing, of course he's …
Susie	Tell me about him.
Richard	Yeah, he's, well, he's a real looker, isn't he?
Louise	Yeah.
Richard	He's a real looker, doesn't look like me, that's for sure, big blue eyes.
Louise	[*Laughs*]

Richard   I mean he's, yeah, I mean he is a little bit on the chubby side, she could feed him a bit less, but I'm not being overly …

Louise   Oh shut up. [*Laughs*]

Richard   Well, you could, I mean, last, you don't want a … do you know what I mean, well, we don't want him to get fat do we, no, anyway.

Louise   He's ten months old, Richard.

Richard   Na, he's got a beautiful smile, hasn't he?

Louise   Yes he has.

Richard   Yeah.

Susie   How does he make you feel?

Richard   Well, I don't know, a mixture of things, like, I love him but I also feel slightly intimidated by him and, you know, I am afraid he's so fragile, sometimes I don't know if I'm gonna … do you know what I mean?

Louise   Someone said to me that they're indestructible and that was really useful, they said that really early on and I keep thinking about that.

Richard   They? Who's they?

Louise   Well, I can't remember, it was someone at the hospital or at the ante-natal group.

Richard   Alright.

Louise   But, oh sorry, that kids are indestructible?

Richard   I don't agree.

Louise   That babies are indestructible.

Richard   But they're not indestructible.

Louise   Well they pretty much are, I mean …

Richard   Well they're not.

I'm clocking Richard's concern that in his bewilderment and frustration he might fear that he could hurt the baby.

Susie   OK, but let's go back to, because you are talking about the feelings that any parent would have thinking about the fragility, and the preciousness and the delicacy and needing to get to know this person.

Richard   Yeah.

Susie   And how, as you say, if you are not with them it can feel intimidating, and you can't know how your hands are going to sit around them and hold them.

Richard   Yeah exactly. I don't feel like me and Isaac are in tune at the moment.

Susie   So when you get up in the morning, where is he?

Louise   He is in the cot by the bed.

Susie   By the bed.

Richard   Yeah.

Louise   On my side.

Susie   Alright.

Louise   Because I feed him, so it's easier for me.

Susie   OK, and how would it be if after you fed him, Richard had him for a bit in the morning. Could you manage that, Louise?

Louise	Well, I could manage that but Richard …
Susie	You know, you have a shower, you leave them to it, you don't engage, you separate yourself out. You don't survey, you don't make sure he's doing it right, you let him figure it out.
Louise	OK, we could try it.
Richard	We'll try that.
Susie	Twenty minutes or so.
Louise	Yeah, he'd have to wind him though, but yeah.
Richard	Wind him?
Louise	Yeah.
Richard	What, you mean pat him, pat him on the back?
Louise	Yeah, you know what I mean, yeah.
Susie	Yeah, but what do you feel when I say this, when I make that suggestion?
Louise	I do feel a bit clingy towards the baby, um, and I also feel that I would really like to spend more time together as a family, but I understand the step towards doing that is for Richard and Isaac to have more one-on-one time, so that seems a constructive way. Can I also say, though, as well, I find it really, I find the mornings really difficult because I miss, I miss Richard in the mornings because the mornings, before we had a baby, before I was pregnant, it was always a time that we would be intimate and that's gone, and by the night time I'm so exhausted and, oh, we've probably had an argument so that isn't going to happen by the night time, so I feel that …
Richard	Yeah.

Louise	I don't feel particularly precious, I feel needy in the mornings as well I think.
Susie	Aha.
	[Pause] Is it strange for you to hear that actually Louise misses you too?
Richard	Yeah, because it doesn't, you know ...
Susie	Doesn't come across?
Richard	Doesn't come across.
Susie	OK, so she's saying it now.
Richard	Yeah, right.
Louise	Because I do really want to make it work.
Richard	Yeah.
Louise	And I think we can, but I feel sometimes that you don't think that I'm on your side, but I am, but I have to protect myself as well and if I need to go back to work because it's a really good opportunity, then I want you to support me in doing that and when you don't I just find it really unattractive.
Richard	I get what you are saying, I do understand what you are saying, and maybe I'm a bit old-fashioned, or can be.
Susie	I think you could be using 'old-fashioned' because you have got these difficult feelings about not knowing how to do it and feeling left out and missing Louise, and not realising that she misses you, and being a little bit frightened of this little bundle and what to do, so I think that is a way of describing all those feelings and when you ...
Richard	Yeah, maybe, the thing is, I get in, I feel like I'm in these

cycles and the cycles are getting longer, whereas before I'd get, I'd get in a head space and it would be, you know, four or five days of feeling a bit down, a bit depressed and then it would pass, whereas I feel like the cycles of feeling in that head space are getting longer and longer.

Louise Are you saying you're depressed?

Richard Well, I don't know if I'm depressed but you know …

I can't tell from Richard's tone how serious this is. The words in themselves are concerning, but they are delivered nonchalantly.

Susie Is it confusion and neglect and not knowing how to spend time together? Louise, you've taken to parenting much more easily because you are at home and you are breast-feeding and you had the support, and it's very hard to know how you are going to have time except doing something at the weekend when you know the baby is napping, because they do nap.

Louise Umm.

Richard Yeah, it's so, yeah, it's like military, isn't it, it's just like so many routines.

Susie Yeah.

Richard It's just like life becomes a routine and you are just trying to be a person in and around the routines, but you don't feel like a person any more, I just feel like it's alarm clocks, it's kind of spreadsheets and you know, getting up, going to bed.

Louise But they all say that that's the best way to do it.

Susie The more engaged that Richard is in being with Isaac, the more it will bring you something rather than just feel like it is taking something away.

Louise	Um.
Richard	Yeah.
Susie	Because right now you are in the alarm clocks as opposed to the richness of, oh, this lovely person who's ours, who we are nurturing. It is a terribly difficult adjustment.
Louise	Um.
Richard	You know, but I just guess I'm, you know, a little bit concerned about maybe repeating what my, the way my father just ran away from the situation. I feel like I'm starting to understand a little bit more maybe why he did that, in a way I can see how a man can feel marginalised in his own family. I'm not justifying why he left but, yeah, I mean I guess I've been reflecting on that.
Susie	That's so helpful, Richard, to know what's going on inside you, because that gives you some space to think, to let Louise know how difficult that is and how the two of you can make it possible, because both of you have to give up things. Louise has to give up the total control in order to find a way to let Richard in.
Louise	Um.
Richard	Because the thing is, I wasn't really going to say it, but I had a moment on the building site last week, I didn't really want to say anything because, you know, I didn't know if it was grounds for like, I don't know what the procedures are, which is why I thought some one-on-one time could be good, but yeah I just had a, I don't know, I just had a bit of an urge to do something and I was quite worried about that.
Susie	Uh-huh.
Louise	Like what?

Richard   I don't know, I was just stood there thinking how would it
be if I just, you know, just jumped out of the window, to
be fair.

Susie   So you are feeling really helpless.

Richard   Yeah, I just thought, you know, I don't know, I just thought,
yeah, I just kind of had the urge to, but I mean I didn't, but
I just had a moment.

Louise   But you can't do that.

Susie   Louise, I imagine it's hard to try and listen to how pushed
out and even desperate Richard feels. This sounds similar
to before. Richard has a very dramatic way of expressing
things.

I hear what he's saying as a request, or it's an ask of how do I get
that, how do I make this, how do I connect with Isaac, how do I
connect with Louise.

Richard   You think that will maybe stop that kind of feeling, stop
that feeling in the void, bring me back to something?

Louise misses what Richard is saying, but she is able to share some
of what's important to her.

Louise   Well, I find it difficult to relate to because I don't feel at the
moment I have an option to leave.

Susie   I understand, Louise, that you are full up here, and now
you are hearing that Richard doesn't know how to be
there and part of you wants him to be there.

Louise   Yes, and it's only, it's only a part because sometimes I feel
that I can't, I can't take on any more needs.

Susie   Uh-huh.

Louise   I feel spent most of the time. Work's different, work's given me something other – in fact it's given me emotional respite, so I suppose that's why I need it and I want to pursue it. Um, well, OK, what do you think?

Richard   I mean …

Louise   What do you think?

Richard   Well, you know, I'll take the Friday off, I'll take the Friday off and you know …

Louise   Well, could you do that?

Richard   Yeah, I could take the Friday off and …

Louise   But really think about it, because I don't want you to just say it here and not having thought it through, but if you could do that, I would make sure I give Isaac to you for that day.

Richard   Yeah.

Louise   And then you get the bonding time with him, but would you really do that?

Richard   Well, yeah, I said I would, didn't I?

Susie   May I make a small suggestion, apart from the early morning, that for two weeks you take a half day off and then you go to the full day, because it's a lot?

Louise   Um.

Richard   Yeah.

Susie   And you might feel safer.

Richard   So what, see how we go, I mean, what are we going to do? You've got a promotion.

Louise   Well, that wouldn't start for six weeks anyway, so you've got six weeks left in which to build some …

Susie   You mean because you would be around but you would go off, for some of the time.

Louise   I could leave you for, perhaps this week for a couple of hours on Friday morning, and I'll go out, I'll go out the house.

Richard   Alright.

Louise   For two hours.

Susie   I don't know whether you want to come back together, I think it would be preferable.

Richard   Yeah.

Louise   Um.

Susie   And I think it would be good to be able to track how this affects you, because actually it is about you as a family as well as your own individual things.

Louise   Yeah, I think that's one of the problems at the moment, I don't feel, I don't feel we've quite got the family.

Susie   OK, so we want to try and get that in train, and in a way we need some evidence of what it is like for you to spend time with Isaac.

Richard   Yeah, that needs to happen, I need to build something with him, because at the moment I am not really sure whether that is going to be possible.

Susie   Of course.

Richard   Well, I am sure it will be possible, but the way I am feeling at the moment, certain things coming out for me, I am not really sure, I am a little bit concerned about my feelings towards him, and I shouldn't be having those kind of feelings towards my own son.

Louise   No.

Richard   So.

Susie   Yeah, but what's important is that you've been frank, and these are things that we can talk about together. And if it's right that you will need one-to-one, we'll figure that out, but in the short term I think we need you to be engaged with this little boy.

Louise   Um.

Richard   Yeah.

Susie   With this little baby, actually, because the sooner you get to know him, the bigger the difference and I think it will shift things, so let's meet very soon and let's have had a little bit of experiment in between.

Louise   I didn't know what to do with him when he came, when he was first born, and I only know what to do with him a bit more because I have spent more time with him.

Susie   Yes, that's very valuable for Richard to know.

Louise   Um.

Richard   I know.

Susie   Because it doesn't come without spending time.

Richard   Yeah, I'll get one of them things, what do they call it, a little strap-on thing.

Susie   Yeah.

Richard   And take him out with me.

Louise   We've got one actually.

Richard   Take him to the …

Louise   To the porch.

Richard   Teach him how to play snooker and all that stuff.

Susie   Exactly so.

Richard   Sort him out.

Susie   OK, alright, so I can see you next Monday if you can both find the time.

Louise   Can you do that?

Richard   Yeah, yeah, I'll sort out the … I mean I'm the boss, right?

Susie   Yeah, you're the boss.

Richard   Yeah, thanks for that, yeah, sure.

Susie   OK.

Richard   Alright, thanks very much Susie.

Susie   Where's the picture?

Louise   Oh sorry, have you got one?

Richard   Oh dear, well, you've got a few on the iPhone, haven't you?

Louise   Yeah, hang on.

Richard   On the old iPhone.

Louise   Here we go. It's the thighs I like.

Susie   Oh, yum, squidge, gosh, he's so gorgeous.

Richard   Alright, see you, thanks for that.

Louise   Thank you.

The session starts with complaint, alienation, frustration and disconnection. Louise is in a bubble with Isaac, Richard's mum and work. She's missing Richard, but she is also resentful and yet excited about new work possibilities. Richard is troubled and left out. He doesn't know how to get into the family, and he's scared and depressed. He wavers between feeling pushed out and feeling that he's lost Louise. The dynamic of the man feeling pushed out and neglected and the woman coping is not so unusual in the first year of becoming parents, especially as Louise has Richard's mum to help. The hope is that by encouraging Richard to come in, he will connect to Isaac and Louise, and his sense of futility and detachment will be transformed. For him to do so requires Louise to let go a bit, and there is a hope that they can find a way of enriching their relationship as they begin to coalesce as a parenting couple. Richard's request for one-to-one sessions because of his fear of suicide or leaving is concerning and will be addressed. I don't sufficiently do so in this session. But I'm hoping that what they've heard and said to each other will mean that his desperation dissipates somewhat, but I am mindful that his worries about himself need tending to, perhaps in sessions just for himself.

John

First Session

John's in his sixties and retired. He was formerly a union official on the railways. His second wife left him, and he came to me in despair. I have been seeing him for eighteen months.

He's a warm man with a self-deprecating laugh. At the beginning of therapy he wore his body heavily. He's no small man, but it seems to be all a part of him now. I always hear him huffing and puffing his way up the long staircase to my consulting room. Despite being breathless, he begins to talk before he sits down.

John   Oh, what a lovely day. I felt very happy this morning. The sun – I know it's cold but I love this kind of day. It's crisp, wakes you up. I'm feeling good actually.

Um, I always find it difficult to start speaking, I know it's the way this works … um, um …

Well you know, when I first came here it wasn't, it wasn't me, it just didn't feel right, you know. But it's really worked for me, talking to you … um …

I've never done this kind of thing before, before I met you, and I've talked about things, really intimate things that I've never said to anybody, not even my ex-wife. So, anyway …

Um, that's why I was happy this morning, because I came out and the sun was out and I thought I really, really love this work that we are doing.

Susie   Uh-huh.

John   And I actually wanted to ask you something because … um … I think it was a documentary about therapists I saw and it said – well you know, I come once a week – well, I mean, there's people, it said on this film, that go like every day to therapy, which you know, six months ago, a year ago, I would have thought – I mean, that's ridiculous, indulgent, you know. But then, or rather now, I thought, maybe I *would* like to come more often to see you actually, and I don't know how often you see people but – I mean, it's really releasing me, talking to you, being here, and I'd like to come three, four times a week because there is so much, you know, in here – [*beats his chest*] – that I really want to talk to you about.

I was walking up the hill in the sun and I thought I really want to see Susie, I want to see her more, and talk to her more about all these things, and I'm sixty-six and I felt like a young man coming up that hill.

Susie   Uh-huh.

I don't respond to John's request at this point. I don't explore it further as I sense he will tell me more about this impulse. Coming twice a week could make sense, but I am not sure. The rhythm of a weekly session with time to digest things in between has felt right up until now.

John   And I thought, why not, you know. I don't want to waste whatever time I've got left. I want to, I want to *really* push forward now in my life. And so I want to come more often and I want to – would I, could I see you outside of the room?

I mean, I know I'm probably breaking every rule in the book, but there's things I do in the week – I don't have many friends – I'm not lonely, but I don't go out with people very much, and there's things I see, I go on walking trips, sometimes I see a film, and I think the only person I want to share this with is you.

Susie   Uh-huh.

I didn't see this coming.

Of course, it isn't unusual for a person to want to see more of their therapist. It isn't unusual that what happens in the outside world is played with reference to the therapist.

The therapy relationship can be a site of emotional truths and connections that aren't yet transferred to the outside world, and so the significance of being understood by the therapist can take on enormous power, and, as John says, he wants to share the beauty that he is seeing, the reflections he's having, the experiences he is now bursting with.

John   I know I'm probably not meant to say that and …

Susie   It's helpful when you say what's on your mind.

John   Yeah.

Susie   I think what you are telling me is that it's exciting as well as a relief to feel that you can say what you want to say, and discover what you want to say, and look at things afresh, whether it's in this room or outside.

John   Yeah.

Susie   And you are in a hurry and you want to live.

John   Yeah, yes, because I was just walking around half-dead for lots of time, you know, for so many years … and I want to – I am in a hurry, um, and you know you said there's not such a thing as I am not meant to say and things I probably shouldn't say but I've got to say, you know, I think I love you, Susie, I do.

Susie   Uh-huh.

John   And I know that's wrong and bad and I know it.

I just think about you all the time, outside. And I have felt like this about a woman many years ago but not for a long, long time.

I have thought about it, and I've thought I'll stop myself saying this because it is stupid, but I do, I do love you.

I'm in love with you and that's why I want to be here and I want to see you outside the room, I want to share my life with you and I know, I just have these feelings about you. I love you, it's all I've got.

I was walking up that hill and I thought I've got to tell her, I've got to tell Susie that I am in love with her. So I'm sorry, but there it is.

Susie   I think that's – look, it's important what you've said. I don't want to just put a dagger through everything you have said, but I think part of why this feels really important and special and why our relationship feels so compelling …

John   Yeah?

Susie   Is because, because I am in this relationship to you, I am listening, I am hearing, I am thinking. I'm feeling with you the struggles you are going through. And that, John, isn't something we could transfer to outside of this room.

This is a delicate moment. The whole of the session is delicate. John finds himself enamoured of me, and I have to find a way to acknowledge his feelings without in any way humiliating him. A declaration of love can be embarrassing if not reciprocated in ordinary circumstances, and these are not ordinary circumstances. It's a cliché to say that patients 'fall in love with their therapists', but, like all clichés, there is something accurate about the intensity of the relationship and the feelings that can be aroused (on both sides) because of the intimacy and sealed nature of the consulting room.

Therapists always fall, or at least this therapist always falls, for some aspects of the person they are working with. I don't mean this in a sexual manner but in the sense that a deep affection, a desire to understand and reach the other, a wish to connect and to be helpful are powerful dimensions of my experience. In order to work with someone for a considerable amount of time and to weather the difficulties we will encounter along the way as they endeavour to change, and with the challenges they will throw at me, the fact of affection will count for a great deal.

In John's case, I feel a profound respect for him in his struggle. His warmth has touched me, as has his desire to repair what's gone so wrong. But love in the way he's talking about has never occurred to me with him.

John   But I think it could be with us.

Now we are in classical Freudian analysis territory. Indeed, the development of the talking cure pioneered by Freud and Breuer at the end of the nineteenth century depended on their being able to understand phenomena that occur in the therapy, naming it as a feature of the therapeutic relationship and then using it in therapeutic work.

The phenomenon they called transference describes the often intense feelings an analysand has towards the therapist, stimulated by the therapeutic setting. These include love and longing, but they could also include hate or disregard. Such feelings occur in other quasi-authority relationships too, but what is particular to psychoanalysis is its study of the feelings that are transferred to the therapist and the use that can be made of it.

Transference can be understood as a reflection of what is in the individual's unconscious mind about the nature of the relationship. It is a version of his or her experience about how relationships of close-ness, mainly learned in the family, pan out. But it isn't simply that. The power of early experience shapes the individual's expectations about relationships in such a way that this psychological imprint is unknowingly foisted on to new romantic relationships. This means that one may treat a teacher like a father, or a boyfriend as a mother, without realising it. In new relationships there is often a psychological tussle inside the individual between seeing the loved person, the other, as she or he actually is and the inner and often unconscious imprint that is held of how previous important relationships have been experienced and therefore will or should be.

To complicate the matter further, there is often the hope of a new relationship fulfilling and fixing the hurts and disappointments from before, while at the same time being itself rewritten as an already known relationship.

If an individual has had hard beginnings, love and attachment will not necessarily be straightforward. It could be expressed as over-evaluating the other and not being able to manage when they turn out to be just a person. When the admired one falls off the white steed they are denigrated, but that then becomes speedily forgotten and they are reinstated as the person who can, or could, understand, fix and make magic. The transference then is a projection or a stand-in for earlier significant relationships. The therapist is not seen as their own person, or as a psychological lifeline, but as one whose affection and acceptance are craved.

Of course, the desire for acceptance may be hidden behind porcupine spikes. It may show itself in a testing way through the analysand being irritating or dismissive or contemptuous, or through an excited kind of love. The transference that emerges – and it can change during the course of a therapy – becomes one of the dimensions of the therapy which comes into play. The therapist examines and shares this with their analysand in the effort to clarify the unconscious processes and projections which may occur.

For Freud, the study of a love transference was predictable. He anticipated that many of the women he saw would fall for him. His take on this was illuminating. He saw transference love – about which he wrote a very important paper, which has been discussed and written about by psychoanalysts many times – as a way for individuals to avoid the work of the therapy. By 'falling in love' with the therapist, Freud argues, they refused to see the unconscious processes at work in their difficulties. They 'fall' in order to sidestep, to be rescued by a father figure of authority and warmth rather than investigate the internalisation of the paternal relationship inside their psyche, to be the child and not the father's partner.

I don't believe this is what John is doing. I take his 'falling' as an expression of his delight in finding that he can be understood and can be open to the world again. I see it not as a distraction from the therapy but as an indicator, as he says, of becoming alive again. That it has landed on me is surely because we have established an important connection. I'm thrilled by his 'coming alive'; I treasure it, and it makes the work rewarding. I have every expectation that this desire will be available to him in a relationship that will be possible down the line.

Susie   Do you think it's possible, John, that it is this opening up that you fear losing?

I see what's happening for you, especially these feelings towards me, as what has been provoked by your coming to therapy and that, in time, you will be taking this passion and desire into your daily life outside the therapy.

I think you are looking at it as though it is to do with me rather than what we are doing together, and how it's …

John	Yes?
Susie	… allowing you to feel a different kind of confidence or realness or …
John	[*Crestfallen*] Well, you don't. You don't feel it, do you?
	Um, I … um … I just thought as I walked up that hill, um … I was thinking about all the things we have talked about, the things that have gone wrong, I thought, and I know you, you are saying I am holding you up as a way out of dealing with those things … and I just thought I would say it because I thought it's not just that, it is actually about you, Susie … um, and I thought I have to say it and I thought I can't bear it if she's – [*and now he is crying*] – if she says no. The thing is, I know it's stupid, but I do love you – [*crying*] – Sorry.
Susie	I don't think it's about 'sorry', and it's not that I am not affected or moved by what you are saying.
	I want to suggest that this is about the loss, not just of your daughter Meg, but of your first wife and …
John	Yeah but …
Susie	… your anguish about not being able to bring yourself to them because …
John	I did, I tried to. Well …
Susie	Yeah, but not just you. *They* couldn't either, it's …
John	But that's why we connect so well, it's like, that's what I didn't have with them.
Susie	Yes, but I'm not a wife.
John	I know but …
Susie	I'm not a partner. I'm a partner in the search to help you

find those aspects of you that haven't been able to be alive for you. And you've become interested in your life so that you've become a curious man. You've got passion, a beating heart and your senses and emotions are opened up.

John Yeah.

Susie And I think we have got a lot more time to spend together within this context.

John But I think about you, like in bed, and I'm sorry, I do, I really want to make love to you.

Susie Uh-huh.

John And I ...

Susie But does it make sense if I say, I think that you're wanting to show your gratitude?

I think we can both treasure that and appreciate that you feel very affected by being attached and cared for and thought about here.

John Yeah.

Susie And you know how seriously I take your troubles.

John Yes I do.

Susie And you know, the ways in which we both enjoy the things that have been changing for you.

John Yeah.

Susie But I think that we need to hold this together between us and just ...

John Yeah, um ...

Susie Because it is not going to happen, and I want to continue to be available to you.

John   Yeah … yeah … no, I'm sorry.

You're not going to kick me out or turn me away because this means so much to me, being here?

Oh dear, I feel terrible now. [*Laughs*]

Susie   Can we go at it the other way around? Can I say that it is because of my concern for you that I am doing my job, and this is the best I can be for you, John?

As for feeling sorry or feeling stupid, I know that's uncomfortable and part of what comes up because of what we are doing here as we talk about things.

It's important that you didn't hold back on this because it will have some meaning and it will shake out in a different way which we don't yet know.

John   Yeah, yeah … Um …

Susie   Let's meet next week as usual.

John   Yeah, OK, OK, we'll meet next week.

I'm sorry, I mean I'm not sorry and I am sorry, you know what I mean.

I – you know when I first came and I could hardly speak – [*laughs*] – and I was thinking if certain people could see me now they would be laughing so much, John in therapy, what a laugh, and I just didn't know what to say, I had not a clue and I hated – I didn't hate you but I thought, I just felt like you were a teacher, you know, and then I thought this morning, on this sunny day, I thought my God, all these months and now I can't wait to get here and talk to you, and you always said – you were great because you didn't tell me off, and you didn't look impatient, you just said try to speak, try to tell, and I thought this morning well I will … and how wonderful

	that Susie has got me to that place, but it's – well, I thought I would be walking out, I thought I might be walking out and skipping down the steps and …
Susie	John, it would be a disservice to you, to send you out skipping down the steps because you woke up and you felt this and you shared it and then it all happened, because we are doing something that is about the rest of your life.
John	Yeah.
Susie	Uh-huh.
John	Yeah.
Susie	Alright, so I'll see you next week.
John	Yeah, you are my life now, but I'm not yours.
	I don't mean to embarrass you. I'm stupid, I've slapped my wrist – [*slaps wrist*] – I'm not going to go down the river with you, but you are very important to me and I'm glad I said what I did.
Susie	John, I'll see you next week.
John	Yes, thank you, bye now.
Susie	Bye bye.

John walks out quite full. He's disappointed, yes, but not only that. I was surprised by the direction of this therapy session. Yet surprise is what keeps a therapist on her toes. We can never know what is coming because therapy is a subversive kind of conversation which can crackle with energy or fear, despair or hope. We follow the feelings, the ideas, the tempo, the timbre of the patient's voice, finding ways of connecting even when we might, as in this instance with John, refuse what he wishes.

So much of therapy is involved in the view of disillusionment. We listen to what the person says, and how it is said, and we put that together with our knowledge of how the individual is in the room with us. We don't so much pierce the bubble of their narrative as layer it, turn it inside out, look at it from unexpected perspectives, join it with what we know of how the individual has construed his or her circumstances. In this endeavour we move away from a picture of blame – my wife didn't understand me, my parents were cruel or negligent – to a more nuanced story of who they were in their psychological and social circumstances and their capacities.

The structures of class – as with John – also come into consideration, as do all the grand narratives which impact our world and the world of our parents and loved ones, to see how the individual mind, feelings, bodies and sense of self were forged in historic time and social attitudes. This moves us away from the view of the innocent and towards more complexity and a curiously enlightened disillusionment. This enlightening disillusionment enables the individual to be in a present without fantastical ideas about who they are or how hard done by they were. They can inhabit their history in new ways and have a richer present.

Second Session

We are four months on from our last session, in which John declared his love for me and his wish to see me outside the sessions. We have worked steadily together since then, with most discussion about his estranged daughter, his early family life and his marriages.

Susie	Hello.
John	Oh, hello, it's John.
Susie	Hi John.
John	Hi Susie, what a lovely day.
Susie	Gorgeous.
John	I'm a bit puffed. I'm a bit embarrassed today.
	Um, you see, the thing is, I've met somebody a few weeks ago and I need to talk about it, I haven't told you yet, but it's been playing on my mind, I think I've got to tell you, because I feel a bit ashamed telling you really.

John has recognised that when he is embarrassed or reluctant to share things with me, it is a signal alerting him to what he needs to speak about. What comes out is a great rush of words and ums.

John	I met this girl – Heva, she's Polish – and it's how I met her that I'm embarrassed about with you. We haven't really talked about sexual things very much and, um, I ah, I think I need to now, you see she, um, because I think you might disapprove of me, and this relationship with Heva, this girl. I need to talk about that as well, but, um, I'm rather frightened of your being angry or disapproving of what I've done, um, because she – you know, I met her

in a massage parlour. I didn't actually, I met her in a café first, but then I saw where she worked and I didn't mean to go in there, um, and I didn't but she kept, the way she smiled when I was just chatting to her in the café kind of haunted me and I thought well the only way I am going to see her more is to go into this place, which I did, two days later, and I was thinking, you know, I am just going in there to talk to her, to, uh, but that's not the way it worked and, um, anyway, then after that night I've, we've seen each other quite a lot the last three weeks, and, ah, she is a lovely girl. I'm also embarrassed because she is much younger than me, obviously, and um it is getting to a point where I have to, um, make some decision about it really because she wants to be with me, I think.

She's got a little boy, eight years old, who I've, who I'm very fond of actually, but she wants more than I am giving her really, or can see myself giving to her, um, although I am very fond of her, she is a lovely girl, um, but I thought, um, the last couple of sessions since I've met her I haven't mentioned it, just because I felt ashamed and I'm a bit frightened of your disapproval because what you say means a lot to me and I feel like I've been a naughty child, you know, and as though I'll be punished, um, um …

Susie   What's the naughty part, is it the meeting somebody, is it …

John   No, it's the way I met her, it's like paying for that.

Susie   Physical comfort and sexual release.

John   Yes, yeah.

Susie   Uh-huh.

John   Physical comfort, yeah. And then, you know, I keep saying, well, I pay for a bottle of milk, I pay for bread, I pay you for this, I pay to ride on the bus, why shouldn't I pay for that, but then it's, it doesn't really work, because I know that area is very difficult and I can't quite ... you know, you are famous for being a feminist, and I grew up, I've met a lot of feminist women, I was always part of that consciousness if you like, you know in the Labour Party, in the unions we were all trying to be correct and respectful to women and um ...

Susie   Well that's lovely, John, but could we take that as known between us and would you just try and tell me what's happened. You were haunted by her smile, you went to the parlour.

John   Yeah.

Susie   Have you been going to the parlour a lot, or you see her outside of the parlour?

John   No, I see her outside, yes. I only went that once.

Susie   Right, OK, so can we just lift off the judgement for a second so I can understand the dilemma you are in?

John   OK, right, because I do need to, I do need, yes, I need to talk to you about that. Anyway, it's kind of ironic because, as you know, I've, I've been wanting intimacy, closeness and I have found it with this girl, I mean it is only weeks, but she is very giving, she is very, and now I'm feeling I want to get away.

Susie   Uh-huh.

John   But I feel guilty, I feel bad because she is sort of depending on me now, and um ...

Susie   Can you help me understand how that happened in two weeks? How did she move from the two of you having a romance to her being dependent on you? Is that what is happening, or what you fear occurring?

John   Yeah, well it's not happened yet, but I can feel it coming.
                  She's, um, her little boy. A lot of it is about her, about
                  the boy, and I think she has very quickly seen me as
                  though she was waiting for somebody like me to come
                  along and she says, you know, you're not like most of the
                  twats, excuse my language, that she met in that massage
                  parlour, she said most of them are drunk, young and
                  stupid, and I despise them.

                  I represented a sort of different kind of client really, and
                  because I wanted to talk to her and to find out about her
                  as well as anything sexual, she, um, she sort of fell for that.

Susie   Aha.

John   You know, like a drowning man to a plank. I think she
                  sees me as her saviour, and she – I mean, she's had a lot of
                  trouble in her life. The father of the boy is this appalling
                  drunken bully who is still in Poland, and she wants to get
                  out of the work she is doing. She is just doing it because it
                  pays her well. She is not really qualified, so she can't get a
                  professional job, and, um, yeah. You know her grandfather
                  knew Lech Wałesa.

Susie   Yes?

John   She's from Gdansk. And when she told me that, I thought
                  bloody hell, this is like the socialist paradise, you know
                  the intimacy and the history and the politics but, because
                  I had been to Poland before and I had done a tour of the
                  shipyards and he was like, what happened with Solidarity
                  and everything,

Susie   Uh-huh.

John   It was like, so it was like I was tapping into this wonderful
                  piece of my life.

Susie   Uh-huh.

John	And, but then we had one of our first arguments the other day. She can't stand Lech Wałesa – she thinks he's dreadful, lying, old-fashioned, old party hack, and to her, that struggle, Solidarity and that part of the history of her country, it doesn't mean anything, and, um, so we had this row, I mean, and I felt very alienated.
Susie	Uh-huh.
John	Although I am very fond of her, I think, I can't keep going down this road. She wants to move in, she wants us to live together now. And she wants me to be like a father to the boy, or grandfather even, and he's a lovely, he's a lovely lad, I am very fond of him, we've done a couple of things together but I'm thinking, I can't, ah, I just think we would have a lot of rows because she's half my age.
Susie	Uh-huh, but …
John	And, um, she wants to do things, I know she does, you know, that I have no interest in, and she has curbed that because she knows who I am, but I think that would be, if it went further, it would be awful.
Susie	But do you think that what you might be embarrassed about with me is that you forgot your own needs in this, that you were taken over by being interested in her and her interested in you, and that maybe you don't quite approve of where you've got to in this, not in terms of the massage parlour, but getting in so far, so quickly?
John	Yes.
Susie	And not having your own eye on you, or ear on it. Does that make any sense?
John	My own ear on me and what I need, you mean?
Susie	Yeah.

John   Yes, but yes, that does make sense. I mean, if I am honest, I have been married twice. Over the last few years I've had a few disastrous dates, dates with various women. My first wife left me for somebody more artistic. My second wife left me because, well, to tell you the truth, I don't quite know. Anyway, the whole love, sex situation is a disaster area for me, *ha*, and um, it's like it's broken and, you know, I am not getting younger and you feel, you think bloody hell, is that it? All this thing that people write about, and talk about. And you see films about how it is to be sexually with somebody who you are politically, intellectually, emotionally connected with, and I was thinking the other day with Heva, I thought it's not going to happen. For a moment I thought, oh, maybe it can happen with a woman half my age, and then I thought, no, it would be a disaster like all the other times, so I think what I'm saying is, you know, my ear on my own needs.

Susie   Uh-huh.

John   Err, it's kind of um, coming up deaf, *ha*. You wrote that book *Impossibility of Sex*.

Susie   Uh-huh.

John   Well, to me that says it all, that title says it all, it's impossible, *ha*, I mean not just sex but like relationships that include sex. *Ha*, it's impossible, and I suppose what I'm worried about, what I'm feeling now, I mean I did feel embarrassed about how I met her because I thought, oh God, Susie is going to like think I'm scum, um, er, for paying for sex, um, but because it was like, I read somewhere in a book, it's like somebody had met a girl, I think it was in the Far East, it was something like this, like a Thai girl in one of those sex places in Bangkok and they developed a relationship and it was very romantic, and he said it was as though he had found the most beautiful orchid growing in a heap of dung, *ha*, and I thought yes I understand that, how beautiful. It doesn't matter where you meet, and I thought this girl, Heva, with her history, with her family, with the way she smiles, she is a very lovely, very lovely woman. And I thought is this a flower that I have found in a, you know, like in a dirty corner of the farmyard sort of thing, and then, well, after this row we had, it was like, no, it's just another nettle, not her fault, I'm not blaming her, it's not her fault, it's just I can't do the love, sex, romance thing, it's the impossibility of …

Susie   So you felt very engaged with her.

John   At first I did, yeah.

Susie   And then you were really disappointed to discover that the Poland and the grandpa that you have an affinity to bears no relation to her desire as a young woman of a different generation who is over here and looking to capitalism …

John   Yeah, well she …

Susie   She's not on the same page. You had an encounter, she is lovely, but you're disappointed that it can't go further.

I am not sure why you are throwing the whole idea about relationship, love, sex out the window. Perhaps this could have been like a little something for you. You didn't sign on the dotted line to look after her and her son. You had an encounter.

John   No, I didn't.

Susie   You had an encounter.

John   Yeah, no, that's fine. I suppose it's like it's the disappointment in me really.

Susie	Uh-huh.
John	It's not … I felt bad the other day because I knew really that it's not really the right thing, and it would be a source of unhappiness in the long run, like with my previous wives.
Susie	But it is reassuring that you *could* hear. Maybe your ear is much more open, maybe you could see that the discrepancy between your desire and what is actually on offer is allowing you to take a pause and think.
John	Yeah, but I mean I'm of an age, that would make sense to me if I was like her age, *ha ha,* if I was thirty-four.
Susie	You might not be able to think that at thirty-four.

We are talking now of a developmental leap. John is grappling towards the notion that he could become stirred up and excited, but in the face of things not fitting he doesn't have to gloss over the differences between them. He can feel his disappointment and not trap himself or Heva.

John	I know – well, I didn't – but now it's like, well, if I keep postponing, I'll be dead, because it hasn't worked out, none of them.
Susie	Well, we are not talking about meeting a woman a week and going nuts over her and it all folding together neatly.
John	No, but I don't think …
Susie	We survived your having a crush on me.
John	Well, yeah.
Susie	Now you've got a crush on somebody else. You were very drawn to somebody, and that made you feel presumably

like you had things to give and alive in a certain kind of way, so now we are pressing the pause button, to get closer to what you are wanting and what might work for you.

John   Yeah.

Susie   I'm not saying it would be easy but …

John   Yes, yes, you remember when – I'm embarrassed again now but, you know, my crush on you?

Susie   Uh-huh.

John   Um, you know when I said I wanted to take you places *ha ha*?

Susie   Yes.

John   Well, I took Heva down the river on a boat to a little pub in Deptford, with dinner by candlelight, I did that with Heva, and, ah, I felt, it was funny, I felt a bit guilty because I really had wanted to take you there.

Susie   Your saying that is helpful, because it's showing us that you've got a parcel of desire or need, a longing to give, or share, but instead of it being bespoke to the person, it got transferred from one to the other.

John   Yes, that's right.

Susie   And what I think we're trying to work on together is, what might make love possible rather than impossible. What's the texture of relating, what is the thing between this person and me, rather than what is a generic love affair.

John   Um.

Susie   And what you've done in two weeks is to experiment, to try to get to know somebody and …

John   Yes.

Susie   And find them charming and lovely, but maybe not for you.

John   Yes.

Susie   Rather than you're not for her, she may not be for you.

John   That's right, yes. I think, I think it's, um, I just felt a sort of, not despair, that's too strong a word, but a sort of realisation that when you get to a point in life, it is not just the number of years, you think, I've had all my chances. I know you don't know what's going to happen tomorrow, but I think, I think, how did that happen that I've, I mean, you see, I can go out tomorrow and I can, all these internet things and hundreds and thousands of people you could meet, one of whom might be the right one, but I'm kind of feeling it's pointless, because the effort of, um, I thought I really wanted it, you see, like I thought I really wanted to explore that and, ah, meet lots of people and renew my life, but actually this isn't it.

                I just feel like, oh give up, what's the point.

Susie   Well, is there a place between giving up and meeting hundreds of people?

                Can there be a place that goes, oh, I felt that desire and that feeling of connection and understanding with Susie, then I risked feeling something with Heva, but actually, perhaps there wasn't quite enough commonality? That's like going out and feeling your way. It's not the roulette ball that lands on the right number the first time.

John   Yes.

Susie   We could be discussing it from the point of view that you're avoiding something with her, and maybe you feel that *is* what is going on, but I hear something else, John, which is if I can't get it right the first go, then I might as well give up.

John   Yeah.

Susie   And maybe, but …

John   Yeah.

Susie   I think what's important is that you have noticed your needs, and you noticed when it didn't fit for you, when you didn't want to stretch. One could stretch with someone whose politics might be different, of course you could, but you would have to have an awful lot going for that to happen.

John   Yes, yes. I've just thought of something.

Susie   What's that smile?

John   Well it's a funny thing. [*Laughing*] I read this book, um, *The Magus*, have you read that book? It's a wonderful book, set in a Greek island. The main character in it is talking. He's like the mentor, guide, wise old man to the young Englishman who visits the island, and I can't remember how it comes up, but he says there was a chap who came to live on this island on his own. He had no family, he bought one of the little disused cottages on the coast of this island and he kept a herd of goats and they lived in the house with him. He was not social, somebody delivered his food, and he was occasionally visited by the old man who's narrating the story, and they would talk occasionally, and it was just this chap with his goats and that was the only family he had, and the chap who was telling the story says he was the happiest man I've ever met. It makes me smile and it makes me sad all at the same time.

Susie   Uh-huh.

John   And it's like, I think actually if I was in a cottage in Derbyshire with a dog, I would be quite happy, but if I got there, I would be sitting there and I probably wouldn't be happy, you know, but this story of this book, I understand that. He loves his goats. That's all a man needs, and I mean he doesn't do anything dirty with them, it's like, it's just they're his friends.

Susie   Yeah.

John   And all the striving and the, you know in *The Impossibility of Sex*, it's like, it drives me mad sometimes, I think just go and live with a dog, but that's because I'm of an age, I'm getting a bit tired of it, that's what it is, and the thought of having to go out again, as it were, and look more, it is a bit exhausting really.

Susie   Well, could we take a pause really, I mean we need to stop in a second anyway.

John   Oh right, OK, anyway, but the first thing, sorry, you must talk.

Susie   It's more important that you do.

John   Yes, I see. Let me say you are very important to me and I thought the main thing was, um, I just felt a bit ashamed because of your judgement, you see, that's my fear, because I feel like I have betrayed something.

Susie   Because you got involved with a sex worker.

John   Yeah, yeah.

Susie   Well, you know, politics has moved on a bit.

John   Yeah, well.

Susie   I am sure you know there are a lot of different views about, but is that the issue, or is it that you're embarrassed that you actually fell for somebody and that in doing so you were betraying our relationship.

John   Something like that, yeah.

Susie   Uh-huh.

John   Something in that area.

Susie   That you sort of see us as being on the same page, with the same ideas and sensibility.

John   Yeah, that's right, yeah.

Susie   Uh-huh, and that maybe you thought I wouldn't want you to find something else for you.

John   Yes, that as well, yeah, yeah, yeah.

Susie   Uh-huh.

John   I felt guilty.

Susie   Uh-huh.

John   Ah yeah, um, yes, that's it really. Yeah, all of them, the women I've been connected with, um, this is going to sound wrong, [*laughing*] it's like I should have been with Susie, or else I should be like that man on the island with his goats – sorry to compare you to the goats, but do you know what I mean, it's like …

Susie   Well, I think what you're saying is you want to be able to match what you're feeling with somebody who you think is listening and feeling it for and with you.

John   That's right.

Susie   And if you're not going to have that, can you find some peace in another way.

John	Yes.
Susie	And the last thing you need is a jangle.
	Look, can we leave it there for now, I know there are a lot of threads open.
John	Yes, yes, right, well I shall see you next time, and yeah, thank you.
Susie	OK, see you next week.
John	Yes, thank you Susie.

John's interest in Heva has opened up confusion and questions in him about longing, connection and morality. His concern that I would (a) disapprove and (b) feel betrayed are important subtexts to the session which we couldn't take up fully but which I know we will return to again.

Therapy can be just like this: an issue is raised but not able to be explored in detail at the time. A drop or two is said which opens up a space for thinking and feeling about the issue to commence before the dilemmas return, which they will do, either with clarity or with greater complexity. They are discussed further, and then understandings can be assimilated. In ordinary conversation we often seek to tie things up with a bow, but in therapy things are allowed to dangle and this isn't a shortcoming but a way in which psychic structural change occurs.

Third Session

The following week.

Susie   Hello.

John   Susie, it's John.

Susie   Come in. The weather is still miraculously lovely.

John   Isn't it? I love it, I love it, yes it's beautiful, it reminds me of, something about a sunny day like this, it's about childhood, I don't know why, but days out with my parents, it takes me right back there, but in a happy way, like a good memory.

Susie   Uh-huh.

John   I was thinking that a day like today, the sun on these beautiful trees in your garden, walking up the road, it's like it takes me right back to a very happy place – today anyway it does, to childhood memories of going out for a picnic with my mum and dad, and my brothers. The weather can do that sometimes, it just takes you straight back to a place. Anyway it's good, it's a good feeling, it's a good feeling, and I feel good because I've made some decisions, Susie, since last week, and I want to, I just want to run them past you because it's coming from a good place. It's not like I've gone mad, or I'm doing things on impulses, running around like a lunatic. It's come to me quite slowly since the last session. It's kind of what you said but it's also what I said … at first I didn't hear it, but now I do, about having an ear on my own needs.

I was thinking, well, I've been feeling that I can hear something now, and some things became very clear, that I want to do, but I want to see if you agree.

I'm going to see Heva tonight actually, and I'm going to tell her it's not going to work out the way she would like. It's going to be quite difficult because I think she's invested a lot of expectation in who I am and what I represent to her, and I'm not going to just pull the rug, I'm going to say I will try and be there for you as much as I can as a friend.

Susie   Uh-huh.

John   So, she's not abandoned, and yes, I'll be there for her, um, as a friend, and then – I'm going to go down to Somerset. This is a big decision. I'm going to reconnect with my daughter, who lives near her mother in Shepton Mallet. I spoke to her on the phone a couple of days ago at the weekend, and we do speak occasionally, every few months, on the phone, and normally it's quite awkward because her mother is a bit anti-me, and the daughter is in her orbit, so it is a bit hard for her. We just kind of exchange pleasantries normally, and this and that, and how are things. She's got a little boy now, who I've seen once, Isaac, and anyway this conversation, it was slightly different, I heard myself saying, Ali, I would really like to see you and your little boy and I'd like to be in touch more, and she – well I was a bit frightened, I thought she might say, oh I don't know because Mum might not like that – but she said yes, that would be lovely, why don't you come down. So that was a breakthrough. I said tell your mother I'll see her as well, just for a cup of tea, just to say hello, there's no agenda, there's nothing going on except I'd like to reconnect with my daughter and see how she's getting on.

Susie   Um.

John   And then the biggest decision is I'm going to move out of

London. I'm going to sell my flat, I'm going to buy a place in Derbyshire. I've been on the internet, I've seen a couple, I know what I want. What I was saying to you last week about living on my own with a dog, I said that as a joke really, a sort of joke, but then since last week, it's become what I want to do, and that's what I meant when you said could I have my ear on something, I had my ear on that actually and it's singing to me loud and clear.

And, yeah, I read this wonderful quote, you'll know it, it's very famous: 'most men live lives of quiet desperation and go to their graves with their song still inside'. And I thought, bloody hell, and it's funny how I kind of knew it but I'd forgotten it, and I saw it the other day, it was in a newspaper and it spoke to me loud and clear, and I thought what is my song, I mean I've been singing a song all my life, but now my song isn't about Heva or the women, or the grumbling around and searching and despairing, it's like to live on those hills near where I grew up, and to be part of that land.

I felt a great joy when I had that sort of epiphany that that's what I wanted, my ear heard that. And then I thought I still want to see you, and that's not a problem, is it?

Susie   Why should it be a problem, John?

John   Right, great, because I shall come down every week, so you will be the connection, a connection.

What do I lose? I lose a lot of what I've been doing – I mean, I'm retired from the union now, but I still do work for them, I still campaign for Labour, I still chair a local meeting, the Labour Party I still am politically connected to, just as a private citizen really, and I am going to lose all that.

Susie   Um.

John   Now, I feel guilty about that, because it is part of who
I am, and what my dad was, and what I believe in, but
I wanted to ask your opinion really. I mean it's like, it's
morally selfish what I'm doing, um, but do you know what,
I'm asking your opinion but in a funny way, I think I know
the answer, because there's parts of this activity that I
take part in, and there's a couple of people that I want to
look after, that's not quite the right word, but there are
a couple of, um, you might say casualties of capitalism,
who are union members who have fallen on hard times
that I have made it my business to look after, in a personal
as well as in a union way, and I can still do that, I still feel
that I can do that, whilst even though, you see the song
that is really playing in my head, the song that's been
playing in my head all my life is community, union, party,
and now the song that's playing in my head is solitude,
peace, countryside, reflection, and it's like a hymn, it's like
a joyful hymn that's playing, I can just see myself in this,
if I've managed to buy it, this cottage, in the Peaks, and,
ah, I mean it's, you know, I feel like it's selfish and it's not
entirely in line with my political values, but I've given my
life to my political values, and I'm not going to drop them,
and I'm not going to drop these people, the important
ones, but I am going to clear out a lot of the routine that
I've been engaged with. I really feel it, I feel like I need to
make that move, it was just after the last session I heard
this trumpet.

As John is sharing his thoughts, they become more elaborated.
He's gone from imagining a move to sketching out how it might
work for him in terms of being able to keep what's important to him
going. It's incredibly heartening for a therapist to see him so active

in relation to his needs, personal needs which he has come to know about over the course of his therapy.

Susie	Uh-huh.
John	Do you think it's selfish politically to retreat from the world?
Susie	Well, that's quite a week.
John	It's a big week, I know.
Susie	I don't think it's got anything to do with selfish.
John	Self, no, ah well, I'm glad you said that.
Susie	I think it has to do with you having a chance to see what might matter to you now.
John	Yeah.
Susie	What you might want to express now.
John	Yes.
Susie	And the memory of your happy times from your childhood which you came in with, and hooking up with those – the fact that you can find that in yourself now.
John	Yeah.
Susie	And the pull to Derbyshire.
John	Yes.
Susie	And maybe what Heva helped you with was to miss your own daughter and your own grandchild, and find a way back to what is central in your personal life. Of course, your politics are totally central to you, but maybe they don't need to be expressed in the same way at this moment.

John   Yes.

Susie   You know, maybe the personal politics and care and connecting with your own child and grandchild and yourself are what this time is about.

John   Yes, I feel, yeah, I think that's right, and I think as long as I keep that connection to the ... I'm thinking of two people in particular, ex-railway men, who have fallen on hard, very hard times.

Susie   Uh-huh.

John   And this is like, yes, the politics is personal. A very fine union man, when I first started working for the union, I asked why are we carrying all this financial burden. To me I couldn't see the logic of it, paying people who were alcoholic – one of them, he'd been in a train crash, it was his fault as well, and he's fallen on very hard times, drink, his family are broken up, he'd been homeless, and the union picked him up and started paying him, and this very fine man, Mick, he said to me, if we don't look after him, then who will, and that's when I became a union man.

            The point is there's two like that, not this chap, he's long dead, but there's two like that and I think my guilt about this idea of moving away from it all was really about those two. There are other people looking after them, but I know they feel a connection to me, and I have to keep that connection to them, and really that's the answer to my problem, because that's the politics of the personal, and I will not abandon them. It's not like I'm going to Siberia, but it's discipline, and it's up to me, because there's going to be times when I won't want to, but I am going to keep coming here, and I'm going to keep in touch with those two men, and I'm going to visit them, and there's times when it's going to be the last thing I want to do, but anyway, I'm rambling now because I've sorted out my own problem.

Thank you for what you said, it's been very helpful and, yes, and personal for me, now, to find out [*beating chest*] something about me, yes and my daughter, and to live in that place on my own … that's fine, it's become, that's the song I am hearing.

So that's what I wanted to tell you anyway, so that's my, that's my … it's been a big week, those are my aims. I think it's practical, it's financially possible, bloody price of property, God in London, it's financially possible and emotionally I feel that's the song, you know, that's the song that's playing now, and it really helped last week, what we said and what you said, about Heva and all of that, it sort of really …

I feel like I've moved on, I really do, and I know we haven't got long. There's one other thing, ahh, which I take with me if this new life works out, I take it with me in my heart to – in my new life. Last week you brought it up, and I was relieved because I didn't, I was frightened of mentioning it, but you mentioned my crush on you, which we, you know, we went through that episode, and we survived it, and I'm still here, we're still talking, um, and the thing like my daughter, all my past, all those relationships, good, bad, good, bad, different times whatever, my children, my son who died, I am taking all them in my heart.

Susie   Uh-huh.

John   And my crush on you, I have to say, Susie, and don't get frightened, I'm not going to go mad, it's not a crush, it's love.

Susie   Uh-huh.

John   And that's one of the things, I've put in boundaries, I hold
             it in a box in my heart, and I shall take that with me and
             I won't mention it, I won't burden you with it, I won't do
             anything, except feel it, and hold it in. [*Beating chest*] You
             see, you're a very brilliant therapist because one time you
             said just hold it, like just very gentle but firm boundaries,
             all the things in our hearts that we can't … that don't go
             the way we want, and um, that was part of the week, I
             thought I've not got over my crush for you, I've not, I still
             feel those feelings, but it's not, you said the word jangle,
             it's not like a jangle, it's just sitting there like a rather
             beautiful thing and it's sort of part of me, and it's alright,
             you know, it's alright, if it's alright for you.

Susie   Well, I suppose how I think about it is, of course it's in you,
             but it's also between us, isn't it?

John   Yes.

Susie   And it's a foundation for going forward, isn't it?

John   Yes, but I know, I mean when I said about the crush, the
             crush in inverted commas, you know I was saying to you,
             because I was thinking I wanted to see you, I wanted to
             take you out, I wanted to take you down the river, you
             know, and as I said to you last week, I went there with
             Heva and it was like I'm doing this thing, and she was up
             for it, you know, she had never been on the river before,
             and candlelit dinner, what could be nicer, but I was just
             thinking this should be Susie, but the difference from the
             last time …

Susie   Uh-huh.

John   … is that I now know it is never going to happen, I know
             we are not going to go out to galleries and films and
             live happily ever after, and it's alright, so I really feel that,

Susie, I'm not trying to give you a therapeutic conversion to make you feel better. It's like I suddenly felt, and it's like your gift to me, because you've made me see that, you've made me feel that, it has taken a long time, it's taken quite a while, but this weekend it was like it's kind of accumulated and I feel it's alright.

Susie   What I hear you saying is, and we'll have to stop on this, is that you trust it enough that you can move somewhere, that you can bear to confront the losses with your daughter and your grandson, and move forward now because you feel you've got something inside and you could even go to Derbyshire.

John   Yeah.

Susie   And hold on to the two guys from the union, even if it is a burden, because you don't feel so depleted, so undernourished, that you have some love inside of you.

John   Yes.

Susie   I think that's what you are saying.

John   Yes.

Susie   So, it continues.

John   Thank you, thank you, thank you very much.

Susie   My absolute pleasure.

John's therapy has allowed him to have a fuller sense of his self and capabilities. When he arrived, he was broken, lost and without a way forward. Slowly we found words together, not so many at first but many by this session, in which he has found a future that interests him. He's felt himself to be a loved human being, accepted and worthy, and that has given him confidence to listen to himself and follow new prompts rather than exist in train lines that fail to nourish. It's been a satisfying therapy for us both. I imagine he will come down weekly for his sessions until they no longer interest him. It has been a privilege and moving for me to work with him.

Natalie

Natalie is in her thirties. She's an estate agent preparing luxury properties for viewing. She and her husband, Josh, are active in their local church community. She's a natty dresser, today in a bright-red fitted dress which complements her rich brown skin. She wears her hair in a short super-curly bob.

It's her third session. She came because she was behaving in a way which disturbed her.

Susie	Hello.
Natalie	Hi, it's Natalie.
Susie	Come on up.
Natalie	Thank you.
Susie	Come on in.
Natalie	Hi, I'm so sorry I'm late. Thank you, thanks. Sorry, rushing. I came, I came straight from work. Oh God, I'm sorry. I always get a bit unnerved when you, when you look at me like that.
Susie	What, with interest?
Natalie	I don't know, um, I feel a bit on the spot.

Being on the spot is of course what one is in therapy, but it's a spot whose aim is to compassionately illuminate behaviour and feelings that seem incomprehensive or counter to one's own interests. With two sets of eyes, ears, minds and hearts on Natalie's predicament we hope to get further than she can on her own.

Natalie	I think I've, I think I've really messed up, in fact I know it, I, oh God, oh God.
	Sorry, I'm OK now, I'm OK. And I missed an appointment at work today; that wasn't good.

Susie   What's occupying your mind?

Natalie   Christopher came back this week and I decided to see
               him. I know that is not a good idea and, um, I met him at
               the house that I was working on today and, um, we got
               caught.

Susie   Sorry?

Natalie   We got caught, sorry, yeah, we got caught.

Susie   Who caught you?

Natalie   Just the people who were coming to sort out the
               chandelier in the house, and oh, you know. I had arranged
               for them to come and clean, and I, I don't know why it
               just went out of my head, it just went out of my head, and
               they came in and we were there and obviously that's not
               OK, so yeah, that happened, and I became a bit flustered
               obviously, and then as Christopher was trying to calm me
               down, I missed my next appointment, so now I have an
               email from my boss asking to speak to me tomorrow.

Susie   Uh-huh.

Natalie   So that's what happened, that's why, that's why I'm late
               and …

Susie   And on the spot.

Natalie   [*Laughing*] Yes, yeah, yeah.

Susie   Well, it seems like a bit of a muddle.

Natalie   I'm all over the place.

Susie   Well, have you got any feelings?

Natalie   Bit scared, if I'm honest.

Susie   Uh-huh.

Natalie   Nervous, confused and I'm always confused these days it seems. It's not OK. What I'm doing is not OK, and I don't know why I can't stop doing it.

She speaks as though she is scolding a part of herself.

Susie   Well this might sound far-fetched, but do you think forgetting the chandelier cleaners was a way of bringing you to reality, because it's quite dramatic, it means you can't just sort of have this affair going off on the side. It's brought you up short and possibly threatened your job as well.

Natalie   Um, if my boss, Charlie, if they tell him, then, then yeah, yeah, yeah, it has, yeah, it has, but the suggestion that I would purposely do this doesn't make any sense.

Susie   Maybe that's too strong. I'm rather asking what use can you make of this unfortunate set of circumstances where you don't know why you are doing this. You forget an appointment and then, because of being caught as you put it, you then forget the next appointment, so things are going out of your head, so …

Natalie   I, I, I know. A wake-up call perhaps.

Susie   Perhaps.

Natalie   Do *you* know why?

Susie   No, Natalie, I don't. I'm interested, I don't have a view, as yet. I don't know more than you know.

Natalie   OK.

Susie   I can help us try and find out.

Natalie   I just, I don't know, I mean it feels like a, a wake-up call, I suppose. I can't keep doing this, I know that much, um, I mean it's silly, it's so silly.

Susie	Yeah. I'm not sure which you can't keep doing.
Natalie	I can't keep seeing Christopher. I can't keep doing that. I have to, I have to stop that, that has to stop.
Susie	And if you imagine stopping it, if you imagine stopping seeing Christopher …
Natalie	I don't want to, I suppose, is the point. That sounds terrible to say out loud.

The act of saying something out loud makes conscious something one may be acting upon but not yet thought about. This is a crucial dimension in therapy where what was previously unknown and as yet unconsidered enters into awareness, enabling the capacity to think about what was under the surface.

Susie	Can we set aside the judgement for a moment? You wince when you say it. You are doing it for a reason because you don't want to not do it.
	You don't want to stop. That doesn't mean you won't stop, but …
Natalie	No, I mean, I mean I have to stop. I have to stop, I absolutely have to stop. I can't, it's not fair on …
Susie	Is it not fair on Josh, not fair on you.
Natalie	Not fair on Josh. He doesn't deserve this.
Susie	Uh-huh.
Natalie	He doesn't. Thank you, sorry.
Susie	One of the things you told me before that I haven't really been able to puzzle out is the fact that you're meant to

be trying for a baby, and yet you're taking the pill and
Josh doesn't know that, and I wonder whether that first
concealment, or that first hidden thing, is something you,
or we, haven't understood well enough.

Natalie   I haven't.

Susie   I don't know if you've understood what it means to say
to Josh, yes, let's try for a baby, and to be unable to stop
taking the pill, while he doesn't know that.

Natalie   No, I …

Susie   So you are already hiding something.

Natalie   Yeah, yeah, I sort of, I guess I thought it just needs a bit
more time and I didn't want to hurt him. We'd agreed,
we'd made an agreement together, and I, I felt like I would
be letting him down somehow, I suppose. We've always
talked about having a family, and I guess you know, we've
been together a long time now, and, um, it should be the
time.

Susie   Uh-huh.

Natalie   Shouldn't it? It should be the time that we're doing this,
and um, I don't know why I can't just do it. I just, sort of,
just need a little more time.

I don't want to worry him, I don't want him to … I don't
know.

Susie   Well, you thought it was better not to discuss it.

Natalie   Because I didn't, I just thought I needed a bit of space. I
didn't think it would go on for so long.

Susie   Uh-huh.

Natalie   And obviously now with …

Susie	Here's what occurs to me. It seems to me these two things might be the same sort of thing. Once you've had a breach, in that you haven't shared something that's important, that creates a separation from Josh, and once you saw *yourself both outside and inside the relationship*, then something else emerged, which is Christopher.
	For example, I'm wondering what the real question you're struggling with is. Is this marriage too much of a constraint? Do you want to stay in it?

Lies are a short cut. They can appear to circumvent a difficulty, but the consequence of a lie is that it can chip away or sever a bond of trust. It can replace connection with moral duty and berating of oneself, as it has with Natalie, and obscure the underlying issues of what not stopping the pill means and why she can't risk talking about this with Josh. Talking openly, even if hesitantly, might allow the bond to hold and strengthen. Lying slices Natalie in two.

Natalie	Yeah, yeah I do. I mean, we've worked so hard.
Susie	Umm.
Natalie	We've worked so hard.
Susie	What does that mean, Natalie?
Natalie	It's, you know, you decide, you make a pact, a decision together to create a life together and not just together …
Susie	But together in a context with the church …
Natalie	Yeah, in the eyes of God.
Susie	And your families and …
Natalie	We made that commitment to each other and to God and you know it's not something you can just throw away, it has meaning beyond the two of us.

Susie	Uh-huh.
Natalie	To throw away all of that, all the work we have done, the decisions we've made, the way we've chosen to live our life, our families.
Susie	So is the birth control sort of playing around with the decision to get pregnant but not letting Josh in on how you're thinking or feeling.
Natalie	Sorry?
Susie	Well, you weren't able to say to him I'm not quite ready.
Natalie	No, because he would have, he would have worried and I didn't want to put that on him. I just needed a moment to think, you know, as I said, I felt like, I'm not making any sense, but I felt like I'd made that commitment to him and, and to God, and I didn't want to, but I know that it doesn't make sense – I didn't want to go back on my word, I know that makes no sense.
Susie	Well, it's got to be making sense somewhere inside of you or it's completely split off …
	[*Long pause*]
Natalie	I sort of felt like he would know.
Susie	Uh-huh.
Natalie	And he doesn't know, he has no idea.
Susie	He hasn't felt the distance, or you're keeping things from him.
Natalie	I don't think so, and I don't know how that can be, why can't he see.
Susie	Two different things could be going on. You could be really good at not showing and he could be really good at seeing things as loving as they've been.

Natalie   Yeah, but if you were, I mean maybe that's …

Susie   And if you think he's missing a beat because you're
              not there on the beat, then I don't know. Do you think
              perhaps he was never on the beat and you just saw him as
              being very much more in tune with you than you are now
              seeing?

I'm intrigued by this sense that Josh is so in tune with her that he
would have picked up her reluctance to get pregnant at this time.
Sometimes we endow our partners with magical powers, as though
they can know us and see us and help us without our telling them,
like parents intuit what an infant needs. But of course, it is rarely so.
Josh's life is busy with his own as well as joint projects, and he may
not have noticed how Natalie has moved away.

Natalie   If I'm really honest, I think Josh has always seen me as
              being better than I really am, and I really try to be that
              person.

Susie   Uh-huh.

Natalie   For him, because he's great, and lovely, and brilliant, and
              caring, and all the things that he should be.

Susie   Uh-huh.

Natalie   And the things that I would like to be.

Susie   Uh-huh.

Natalie   But clearly I'm not if I can do this to him. So …

Susie   Well, what do you think you are that you've been trying
              hard to be? I don't mean with the pill or with Christopher,
              but this idea that you've expressed, that he's always seen
              me as better than I am.

Natalie   The thing that my faith has given me is a guide and a foundation and a way to be in the world that is greater than me. Does that make sense?

Susie   Yes.

Natalie   Um, because you know we are all humans, though of course we, we fall down and um, you know, I've certainly been guilty of that, of course I have, and my faith gives me, it allows me, or I try to be the best version of myself to be, to not get caught in my own selfishness, to …

Susie   Uh-huh.

Natalie   [*Pause*] To appreciate my life as the gift from God that it is and to show thanks for that. That is what I try to do so, yeah, I don't know, you look really confused.

Susie   I'm not confused. What I'm thinking about is the best version of yourself that is this gift from your faith, and I'm wondering how awful you do actually feel about yourself. I don't so much mean because of what's happened today, but you seem to have a sense of not really being as good as you'd like to be, and I wonder what's underneath the good, or the not good.

Natalie   But they're not the same for all of us.

Susie   Well, are you saying that religion or your faith, or religion in general, is a way for human beings to be better than they are?

Natalie   No, I don't think God is there to make us better. That's reducing him to something very small.

Susie   Uh-huh.

Natalie   I don't mean that at all actually, um, you know, he sees everything, so no matter how much you are trying to

improve – you know that won't work if you are trying
to pretend to be a version of yourself. God, of course he
knows, he knows us all so that won't work, it's not like he's
a self-help manual or something.

Susie   No, but he is a God in your head who sees frailties or
errors, and knows whether it's authentic, that's what
I think you're saying and you can't just get away with
things.

Religious and spiritual beliefs, like political sensibilities, are part of
an individual's sense of self, and while they may be unsettled during
therapy, it is the duty of the therapist to respect them. Therapy is
helpful when the individual feels that how they feel and think and
what they believe is understood.

Natalie   No, of course not.

Susie   And that what you've stumbled on in this chandelier/
Christopher incident, and the birth control pills, is not
being able to be straight with yourself or with Josh to
begin with about your own hesitation.

            Isn't God a God of interest as well as forgiveness, not
simply a God of yanking yourself up?

Natalie   Of course, yes, yes, I didn't mean to make it sound like
that, but I mean maybe, oh, maybe I am just lying to
myself and actually it just really serves me – it's just
easier for me not to talk to Josh, to save the difficult
conversation, but that doesn't …

Susie   Well, you feel you were not ready, you didn't want to hurt
him. The not quite ready had a lot of other things in it
which he's excluded from knowing because he doesn't
know that they are going on inside of you. Maybe you

don't know what they are because you've now piled on something else on top of that which adds to the befuddlement, and to your upset.

Natalie Befuddled is a good word. [*Laughing*] I feel befuddled a lot.

Susie Uh-huh.

Natalie I don't know why I'm doing it – I've said that so many times this session, I'm sorry.

Susie Well, I think that's a useful place to know you're at. We're not trying to put you in a square, we're trying to understand. After all, you came because you are befuddled.

Natalie Yeah.

Susie And we need to see it and experience it and not be frightened so that you can hold it in a way until certain strands become a bit clearer.

Natalie Yep, I don't know how that works.

Susie Well, I am not sure it is immediately comforting, but I think there's a lot going on here. It's not just chance – you didn't just stop taking the pill, it was driven by something. You didn't just forget the chandeliers, it was driven by something. You didn't just forget the appointment, it was driven by something. And although that might be very hard to take on, to see that you've got a certain amount of energy in those things, it does give you another way into looking at yourself and looking at what's motivated or pushing these behaviours, and if I've added to the befuddlement by saying that, just say so.

Natalie [*Laughing*] Um, a little, a little, I mean it is very unlike me, but the idea that I would have somehow orchestrated that to turn my life – it doesn't benefit me in any way for my boss to find out, it doesn't benefit me in any way for Christopher, sorry, oh gosh, for Josh, not Christopher, for Josh to find out.

Susie   No, it doesn't benefit either of those, but it might have some value or meaning for you to be able to talk about it here privately, to try to secure your job so you've got that while you figure out if there's another level of meaning going on here, Natalie.

Natalie   Um.

Susie   Because from what you've told me, ever since you gave up your teenage rebellion, you've been a very, very good person.

Natalie   Well.

Susie   And it's been the way you put yourself together. And perhaps some things are not quite who you are now as a thirty-two-year-old on the brink of having a baby.

Natalie   Sorry, say that again.

Susie   Well, the image I get is that when you were a teenager – this is from what you've told me – you kind of smashed up things. You were rebellious, you decided not to go to university, you got caught up in all sorts of things that took you off the road that you thought you might be on, or certainly your parents did, and then you put yourself together and you found a way to work and live, and be with Josh, and it's been good enough, but it's kept you in a sort of casing, and it could be that your interest in the church and the way that you've been so engaged with it, is a way to give you a set of boundaries and morals to live by.

Maybe the challenge is to understand those boundaries

and morals from the inside and in a curious way. It's an act of maturity to have got yourself into this befuddlement.

Natalie   An act of maturity! It feels the opposite.

Susie   Yes, I think it's a bit confusing, but if we go back to that incredible rebellion from teenage, you just sort of turned over a new leaf, you didn't actually take the things that were in that rebellion, and maybe there's something, some pieces of you, that got left out.

I think we probably have to stop there because I don't think we can understand more of it right now.

Natalie   OK.

Susie   And you may think this is a silly framework to consider, but I'm trying to make sense of the befuddlement.

Natalie   Thank you, thank you.

Susie   Ok, alright.

This kind of befuddlement is the bread and butter of therapy. There aren't always neat solutions, and not knowing why one has done something, and the upset it throws up, are part of reaching deeper understandings of your own motivations and conflicts and confusion, so when I say to Natalie let's leave it on befuddlement, I'm reasonably optimistic that there are strands, if we can get hold of, which will give her access to bits of herself she split off quite a while ago.

The theme of lying makes sense to me in terms of Natalie's difficulty with holding together different parts of herself. It is part of what she has done to manage the contradictions. She went from being a 'good girl' to a rebellious teenager to a 'good young woman', but in each of these identities parts of her became severed and split off. The dilemma is how to integrate these different aspects of herself so that her commitment to the church and to Josh (if she wants to stay married) can flourish and that what is constituted in the good can sit alongside the more rebellious sense of self rather than be banished. Her affair might be a way for her to be in touch with the part of her that has been sequestered. At present the seesaw she's on, in which one side of her is exposed and the other side lower down, is failing her. In finding a way to accept these different parts of herself the splitting can lessen.

Jo

First Session

Jo is in her thirties. It is her first session. She bounces in, lively and nervy. She sent me an email requesting therapy, saying only that she'd gone off track. She acts with an unusual mixture of nonchalance and diffidence as she enters the room. She has a London accent, and an expressive face, which is engaging. She speaks at a great pace.

Jo	Hi.
Susie	Hello, I'm Susie.
Jo	I'm Jo. Am I really late? I am so sorry, it's just that I think you gave me the wrong address and I don't normally get stuff like that wrong, which is why I'm late and I think I have now wasted like fifteen minutes or something.
Susie	Come in, just go straight ahead.
	I'm really sorry, it would be a bit unusual.
Jo	Is it in here?
Susie	Yes, would you like to take a seat on the sofa?
Jo	Yeah, oh God, I did not want to start it like this. I didn't want to come in as a wreck. It's just one of those days where everything goes wrong.
Susie	Uh-huh.
Jo	Anyway.

When I meet someone for the first time, I am really interested to hear what they have to say and how they say it. I notice the pauses, the way their voice gets louder or softer. I notice their physical being and I notice their impact on me. We learn a surprising amount in a first encounter about the themes an individual is struggling with and how their mind has construed their situation in such a way that they can't find exit points from their difficulties. As we listen, we are assessing whether we believe we will be able to be of use to them. Therapy is not for everyone. Sometimes just a single session will be helpful.

What is said in a first session does not become set in stone. The content will shift, or something unbidden may emerge in session twenty. But how the individual frames her or his dilemmas will be the opening guide.

Jo is late and she says she has been given the wrong address. I know something has gone awry here because she received my correct address by email. So I am alert to what those two things might tell us about Jo's way of being in the world and being with herself. Jo comes in a bit flustered, breathy and busy, and my ears are open to hear how she gets in the way of herself.

Susie   So, tell me.

Jo   Yeah, yeah, I guess I am here because I am unhappy. I'm an actress, well – God, I say I'm an actress, I'm not an actress because I work in a café. I *was* an actress. I was a successful actress at a certain level but I haven't had any work for ages. Anyway, my drama school is having the big ten-year reunion.

Susie   Uh-huh.

Jo   Tonight. But the thing is, it is happening in the club where I work and I have to work because I need the money and they are short-staffed, and I have obviously known about it for a few weeks and I can just feel it getting worse and worse as it gets nearer and nearer, and now it's today.

Susie   Uh-huh.

Jo   And I am not in any position that I thought I would be. And an ex-boyfriend of mine – he, really, if I am honest, really was the only person who actually understood me – he is going to be there and I haven't seen him for ten years.

I haven't really had anything, a relationship, that even comes close to that, you know, because I am the one that finished it, everything is drained from me. I don't know, I don't even know why I am here because the fact is I feel ridiculous now sat here, having just got upset about an ex-boyfriend, ahh, I feel slightly uncomfortable.

Susie   Uh-huh.

Jo   If I'm honest, right now, because I don't ... Oh I feel ridiculous.

Susie   Well, it can feel a bit ridiculous because you are talking to a complete stranger and trying to give me a picture of the things that concern you.

Jo   Yeah.

I am listening to Jo and I am torn as to what to say to her. I register her panic.

Her words tumble out, and tracking what's particularly important for her – whether it's the ex-boyfriend, or the disappointment in her acting career, or some quite other focus – is going to take a while. Her voice is like a screech, and then she halts.

I am interested in why she was unable to swap her shift, which is a very ordinary thing to do when you are feeling under pressure. But she wasn't able to think that or make the change, and so I am wondering if she is revealing something about the way she inadvertently traps herself.

I feel the intensity of the clamp around Jo's mind. The trap provokes me to think about whether she lives in a story of no exit, of believing she will be the victim. That she will be abject.

When in doubt, a psychotherapist has to keep their mouth shut. The point of therapy is to see how something unfolds. I need to notice the shifts in the emotional temperature as she recounts her story. I am pulled, just as Jo is, into the tension she feels about swapping the shift, or rather her not being able to; seeing her classmates and not feeling successful; and seeing the ex-boyfriend; and I need to wait, to hold on to all of these themes so that I can be of use to her.

Jo   And I don't want people's pity at this reunion tonight, which I know they are going to feel because I see it all the time in people's faces, you can see it.

Susie   You see pity or you see compassion?

             You interpret it as pity. Is it pity?

Jo   Maybe, yeah, I don't – maybe I'm projecting that on to them, I don't know. [*Sighs*]

I am nudging Jo a little bit here to see whether she has any emotional bandwidth.

Jo has used the word 'projection', which is quite useful. It gives me a sense that she might understand that what she thinks and imagines isn't always the case and that she may misinterpret what other people are feeling because of her own difficult feelings about her work life. Her disposition is cheery, highly strung and anxious all at the same time. I feel her slipping between various emotional states within a millisecond. This presumably is her style and I need to respect it, but I also want to find a way to slow her down.

Susie   I suppose the important thing for us is to figure out is how *you* feel about this.

Jo   I am scared where I will end up. I know I keep thinking about the morning that we broke up. We just parted and it wasn't horrible, it wasn't in any way – nobody did anything actually wrong.

Susie   Uh-huh.

Jo   And I just let it go. I can remember it so clearly. I watched him walk, walk away, and actually if I am honest he is the only person that I shared true intimacy with, and I don't know why I gave up on it so easily.

Just in a few sentences Jo has slowed down and moved into a reflective space. She's now looking at me intently. The pace of her words has changed and I'm feeling that I might be able to be of some help. My question which follows may seem rather hackneyed as it diverts her attention to her earlier life. It comes out of the full stop she seems to have arrived at. I could have waited and not said anything, but I was mindful that we only had a very short session and I needed to see what to recommend. She has had the thought that she gave up on the relationship, on him, so easily many times, and is as perplexed now as she was ten years ago.

Susie   And when you think of loss, did you have earlier losses in your life?

Jo   Not really, I don't think so, not that I can …

We are back at another full stop.

Susie   Tell me a bit about your background.

Jo	Well, I don't really know my dad. I didn't know him.
Susie	Is that your phone?
Jo	Oh God, sorry.
Susie	Would you mind turning it off, thank you.
Jo	Hold on a second, oh, I've just got to answer this quickly, I'm really sorry.
	Hello … I um, I'm just at a meeting actually … OK, OK, I'll be there in ten, I'm really sorry, I'm just around the corner.
	Is it OK if I keep my phone on?
Susie	No, I'm afraid it isn't, because I can't really concentrate and we've got such a very short time together and I would really like …
Jo	I'm sorry.

The moment was lost with her and we are sent in a different direction, one that might be very helpful to us to understand as the therapy continues.

We have just talked about the humiliation of the reunion, the loss of the boyfriend and the fact that she didn't know her dad, and I am linking those things in my mind as a possibility. But before I can think about those connections and whether they are relevant, and certainly before she can feel anything about them, we are off on a train in a completely different direction.

Jo	I'm sorry because now I have completely forgotten what we were talking about.
Susie	Uh.
Jo	I'm not very good at this sort of thing. Is there a right way to do it?

Susie   No.

Jo   OK.

Susie   We just have to get to know each other.

Jo   OK, yup …

Susie   Something led you to be in touch.

Jo   Yeah, my friend who comes to you suggested it might be a good idea, I think. I think actually he was just bored of listening to me going on about how awful my life is, so he just suggested that I come in and pay somebody else to listen to me talk.

              Sorry, I am just talking too much, actually I guess that's the point, isn't it, but yeah.

Susie   If I'm seeing your friend, I wouldn't be able to see you.

I am nonplussed about this information as I usually know how an individual has come to me, and I fear I was a little harsh in rushing to say that I wouldn't be able to see her. I wouldn't, but I wish I could have said it more gently. If I examine myself as to why I was so hasty, I think it is probably because the session has been quite challenging so far, with us having so little time and the disruption of the phone. I was too hurried to manage this third piece of awkward information better.

Jo   Oh.

Susie   But I would be able to think about who might be right and recommend them to you.

Jo   Oh, OK. But the thing is, I haven't even – [*sigh*] – I haven't even told you his name.

              I feel like maybe – I feel like, I feel like you just don't want to see me. I know I've just wasted however much money coming here and it kind of feels like you are dumping me! Like I've just, I've just told you what I have got to go and do tonight. Why would you choose to say something like that?

Susie   It's really unfortunate that I didn't know. You knew, of course, but you didn't know that it would preclude me seeing you.

Jo   Well, shall we just call it a day then?

Susie   No, sit please.

Jo   I mean there's no point going on, is there really.

Susie   Jo, please sit down because it's not – there's things that we are in the middle of that I think it is quite worth us trying to just hold on to.

Jo   This is just so typical.

             This is really typical of my life because I can't …

Susie   OK, so that's what's very useful for us, isn't it? If it's typical that something doesn't go as you wish, you have been bold enough to show me what doesn't work. And I would like to think about who would be the right therapist for you.

Jo   But why wouldn't you be the right therapist?

Susie   I might be the right therapist. Of course I might be the right therapist, I might be very interested to be …

Jo   It just feels like you're fobbing me off to somebody else.

Susie   Uh-huh.

Jo   Which I wasn't expecting. I just wasn't expecting this.

Susie   No, I can see that, I can see that that's – it's definitely not

> what you would have wished, but I think maybe in your
> jumping to the idea of why I'm doing it, and discounting
> what I am actually saying by making up a different story to
> yourself, it is inadvertently hurting you, because actually
> – this isn't about you, it is really about me, it's about me.
> It's about how I work and the kind of rules or ethics that
> govern my job.
>
> Even though the impact is hurtful for you, it's not about
> who you are and how it pleases or displeases me.

Jo is, quite understandably, projecting on to me a rejection. This echoes the earlier moment when she imagines her classmates pitying her. It is important to give her the reality here so that she can take back the worry that it is all about how pitiful she is.

It's very interesting when the problem the individual has in part talked about comes alive in a therapy session. Jo's talking about rejection and I find myself bounced into rejecting her. I feel this acutely. Worse, I can't even repair it for her properly, and so I have caused her hurt and added to her chaos.

I don't want to have an abrupt ending with Jo: she's had an abrupt ending with the boyfriend from ten years ago and I am imagining that her father disappeared when she was very little, although I don't have any confirmation of this. I do know that I can't be of use to her if I am seeing her friend. Hearing about her through someone else's eyes, or seeing her friend through her eyes, isn't really the point. Therapy is a sealed environment. We aim to hear things first-hand and then assess them with the person concerned. We look for the discordances rather than hearing them elsewhere. It's not perfect because people are not always reliable reporters of their own behaviour, but we do need to see things from their perspective as we add in ours. Knowing something from someone else does influence one, and although that can be useful, it can also be distorting.

Such rules were hard learned through years of experience in the psychoanalytic journey. Initially Freud and his followers saw people who were friends and colleagues and holidayed with some of them, but as psychoanalysis became a mainstream practice in the United States after the Second World War there was enough accumulated experience to see that friendships weren't the wisest of structures for a practice. It made it all a bit too cosy and sometimes rather muddled.

It's not practicable in today's world to know nothing of one's patients other than what they show and tell. The internet has put paid to that. Then, too, they have information about their chosen practitioner; indeed they may well have researched you before they approach you. They can know a great deal more about the therapist than what the therapist shows of her- or himself through their demeanour in the consulting room.

A therapist might be asked, for example, how her daughter enjoys such and such a college, the patient having discovered through a couple of clicks what university the therapist's daughter has attended. When such information is brought to the therapy, it can have a significance beyond the simple enquiry. The therapist might be interested in why this particular patient has asked this of her and as she enquires about it, the patient might be flummoxed. The question was for her part innocent.

When I say it has a significance, I am not implying that this is misbehaviour or inappropriate on the analysand's part. I'm signalling rather that it can become an additional form of communication in the therapy relationship. A query about a daughter's college could mean any number of things, from the patient's straightforward interest, to anxiety, to a wish to see the therapist's private life as a guide for her- or himself, to a need to show that her or his daughter is 'doing well' – and everything in between. It can sound precious to say we are interested in exploring such questions for what they yield about the patient's inner world, but if used judiciously such an interchange can be productive.

But back to Jo, for whom such questions are hardly on the table. She got in touch without knowing that my seeing her friend would preclude my taking her on for therapy. She knew my name from him and, as it turned out, had found my details through the internet. For her this was an act of responsibility. She looked me up and found out how to contact me. She didn't know what my rules were. My intention now is to find a way of moving her to somebody else if she decides to pursue therapy. I hope she will be able to do this and that our encounter won't sit as another cut-off where she falls through the cracks.

Jo	So, well, what do we do now?
Susie	Well, what I'd like to do is see you again for a full session and see whether you actually want to pursue therapy, and for me to see who comes up in my own mind that I think would be good for you.
Jo	Yeah, I'm not sure that I do want to pursue therapy.
Susie	That's understandable … but perhaps the idea will sit with you.
Jo	I guess I need to think about it. I don't want to make any big decisions because that's what's got me in trouble. Thank you.
Susie	OK.
Jo	And I'll be in touch.
Susie	OK.
Jo	Alright, thanks.

Jo's had a difficult first session, and she has a tricky night to navigate. Despite our difficult meeting, I hope that she will be back for a proper assessment and referral.

A therapist, of no matter how much experience, cannot predict how the words that are said in a session will settle in. It is one of the peculiarities of the analytic encounter: the psychotherapist puts her- or himself out to try to understand the dilemmas the other is grappling with, but we can't know which words – certainly not in early sessions – will resonate. Individuals and couples come to their ensuing sessions having found something illuminating that the therapist may not have noticed had much salience. We can't always calibrate things. The therapist is always increasing, and revising, her or his knowledge and understandings of the person and the way they receive the words shared in the session.

This is not to say that a therapist doesn't know what she is doing. Of course not. It is to say that the human psyche is intricate, surprising, and that while consciously things may make sense, the more unconscious processes are also in train and do not reveal themselves in a logical sequence.

Second Session

It's six months later, and Jo has come for a referral.

Jo   Hello Susie, it's Jo.

Susie   Come on up.

Jo   Thanks.

Susie   Hello Jo, come on in.

Jo   Hi, thanks. How are you?

Susie   Good, thank you.

Jo   Thank you for seeing me, yeah. I guess my memory of the last time that we met, I wasn't entirely I don't think ready for, for what this is actually, and I think I had so much on my mind at the time, that I was slightly ... my memory of it is quite blurred.

Susie   Uh-huh.

Jo   So I just ...

Susie   And also you were very thrown by the fact that I wasn't in a position to see you.

Jo   Yeah.

Susie   And you were facing the reunion.

Jo   Yes.

Susie   And your ex-partner.

Jo   Yes, yes. Yes, and I think that at the time I was feeling quite vulnerable and I think I reacted quite strongly, and I guess I would like to kind of start again, but also you did say that you could refer me to somebody.

Susie   Yeah, of course. Let me listen, let us talk and let's see what's what.

Jo   OK, what it is, is that things have got considerably worse since the last time that you saw me. I don't have a job any more. I was sacked, to be honest, um, and you could say that I am homeless.

Susie   Uh-huh.

Jo   And what's difficult is that the homeless that I know about are people living on streets holding paper cups, but yet I am actually homeless even though I don't look like I am. So at the moment I'm, I've been flat-sitting for some very successful friends who have been out in LA and they come back tomorrow, sorry next week, and I don't have anywhere to go, I don't have, I don't have a home, so I don't have a base and I've been sort of sofa-hopping.

Susie   Uh-huh.

Jo   And it's sort of beginning to make me feel slightly like I'm being left behind in general because I feel like everything I have worked for, whether it be waitressing or whether it be acting, is, um, it hasn't actually done any good. I live in a world where most of my friends have a home, they have children, they have a partner, they have that set-up.

Susie   Uh-huh.

Jo   Which is a set-up that we are led to believe is what you want in life, that's what you work for, that's what you strive for, and I am overwhelmingly aware that I don't have any of those, and I don't know whether it is my fault. I don't know whether I have brought it on myself.

What's impressing me about Jo today is the sadness she feels, which is quite a move away from the fraught, on-edge place she was in when I met her the first time. The seriousness she feels about her circumstances will stand her in good stead because it brings her closer to an important reality. It means there is less of a screen between herself and any capacities she might be able to draw on to get herself out of her difficult situation.

Susie   Uh-huh.

Jo   You know, people say that luck is a huge part of everything, especially in the career that I have chosen and I am trying to have, and I feel like I need to stop and look at myself and change something, because I am getting very cynical about everything, because I can't really see a way out of my situation, which is why I think I need help, and yet I don't have the money in order to get help, I don't know whether you can suggest anywhere to go, anyone to talk to that will listen to me or will help me on that route to, to helping myself I guess, because I have just reached a point where I don't know where else to go and I don't know how to help myself.

Susie   I am hesitating because I don't think money for therapy is the insurmountable problem, there are a few places or people that I might be able to match you up with, so tell me a bit more about the isolation and the fear that you are living with at the moment.

Jo   Well, because I don't have any money to pay rent, my friends are saying, oh you can sleep on my sofa, and I kind of can't keep doing that because I am not a child any more, and these are people my own age, these are friends of mine who have the basics. I don't even have the basics, so I feel like I am floundering, and I don't know whether it's my fault that I have created my own destiny.

Susie   Well, 'fault' is a funny word, isn't it?

I want to lift off the notion of fault for the moment. I'm not advocating a denial of responsibility. The complex manner in which our personal history and circumstances fetch us up in the particular situations they do are important, and need to be addressed, but fault in this bit of a therapy dialogue would seem to operate as a clamp, shutting down what we need to look at in this assessment.

Jo	Yeah.
Susie	Because you are in a very tough spot, and the question is how are you going to find a way through if you don't get a lucky break.
Jo	Yeah, and I feel like that has got so much to do with the industry that I am in.
Susie	Exactly, so that is a real situation, but I'm not sure it's helpful for fault to dominate the conversation. I think we should see a little bit what you feel your capacities are that you are not able to use at the moment. I think the very fact that you are flat-sitting is probably a much safer situation than perching on somebody's sofa.
Jo	Yes, although that is going to come to an end.
Susie	I know, but that is a way that some people manage in the periods that they have difficulty. They become the person who flat-sits.
Jo	I am also aware that it is not my existence that I am living.
Susie	Yes.
Jo	It's not my ...
Susie	Home, yes.
Jo	Home, it's not my million-pound home. I mean, I am literally a guest.

| Susie | Yes, but you are providing a service, and painful as it may be to see the gap between what your friends have been able to put together and how the cookie has crumbled for you. If you could get something in the short term, another place to stay, you can look at the possibilities there are for you as somebody who is a skilled actor who hasn't been able to find work of late and doesn't quite know what to do with that difficulty, and all the things that bubble up inside of you can be spoken and thought about. |

I'm picking up on Jo's anxiety and before she goes into full tilt, but without coming up with a false solution, I want to convey to her a temporary calm place such as another home-sit, to do some thinking from, which is what I am implying in using the phrase that she is providing a service.

Jo	Yeah, I feel like I am living with an increasing anxiety about not only now, but the future. Have I made bad choices? Have I brought this on myself?
Susie	Let's just explore that for a moment; what are the sorts of things that run through your mind when you say, 'Have I brought this on myself, did I make bad choices?'
Jo	Well, I feel like anyone who has ever shown genuine care for me, and love for me, I have sort of pushed them away.
Susie	And would you say that was true not just with your boyfriend? Would you say that was true with directors that you have worked with?
Jo	Possibly.
Susie	Can you think about that a little bit more, because a director is looking after a play.
Jo	Yeah.

Susie   And is also like the head of a family.

Jo   Yeah, something that I have been drawn to in my life is
              the experience of being in that family, but that family
              will come to an end, and that family is everything to you.
              But a year or so later that family does not exist and yet
              everyone, nearly everyone I know, they have a family,
              they have their own family. A few years down the line you
              are not part of that director's family any more because
              that director has moved on, or the other actors that you
              worked with.

Susie   Yes, you have a very intense experience and then it stays
              with you, and then it diminishes, doesn't it?

Jo   Yeah.

Susie   Or it doesn't join up unless you work with those actors
              again.

Jo   But it's not real life.

I am always intrigued when people talk about work as 'not real life'.
Work, if we are very lucky, can be engrossing. Of course, for many
it can be deadening, but thinking about Jo's work as an actor, it was
very real. There she found multiple relationships and encounters,
demands, difficulties, triumphs and boring bits. Work is where
many people thrive, and I sense that it is where Jo felt most fulfilled.

Susie   Well, it was real life. Let me ask you this because I am not
              sure if this is what you are hinting at: do you think that
              your engagement with the director has been in any way
              dismissive, or have you thrown any of that away, when
              you question whether you have brought it on yourself?

Jo   No, I don't think that's the case. I think it is more to do with
              relationships I have had.

Susie   Relationships inside the theatre or relationships outside?

Jo   In real life, in my life, theatre and what I do is everything to me, but when you go home at night …

Susie   Yeah, but how do you understand that you're not working? I know it's chance if you do or don't get picked for a role, so I'd like to divide this into two.

Jo   Oh I see, what you are talking about.

Susie   Because you've said a couple of times: I'm fearful that I have brought this on myself.

Jo   Well, yes, because I don't know how I've reached this point in my life where I have nothing. And I want to change that.

Susie   Part of the not having is the not working, so all I'm trying to understand, and I could be barking completely up the wrong tree, but do you feel if you reflect on it, that when you have pushed people away people who are caring – I know it is a very precious relationship, or an intimate, or a powerful relationship that a director and the players have – is there something you feel you've done to prevent the director coming towards you again?

Jo   Not that I can think of.

Susie   OK.

Jo   Yeah.

Susie   So it doesn't feel like that at all, it feels like in your world outside of the theatre.

Jo   I mean, of course I have other questions like have I gone about the whole thing in completely the wrong way in not thinking about the industry as a business. I have never come at it from that viewpoint, and so I have done some great work and I am proud of the work that I have done, but how is it that I have worked for so long and I have got nothing to show for it.

Susie   You mean that the work has dried up and you're homeless.

Jo   Yeah, should I have gone about it ...?

Susie   How?

Jo   I don't know, have a different personality, because I can't help but compare myself to everyone, you know, around me, and also the idea of having no money, the idea of being skint, you know, you go on social media on Instagram or whatever, and one minute you are having a conversation with someone who's agreeing with you, and going, oh yeah, like I'm super-skint, I'm really skint, and then two days later they are posting photos of them in Barbados on holiday, and I'm just, like, well, I would like to be that sort of skint please, because if you're skint, then what am I, because I don't come from money, my parents don't have anything to give me. I guess I'm just, I'm just feeling very cynical about the whole thing and I don't want to. I want something to change and I don't know whether it's – for example, I expected the reunion to go badly, and it did go badly.

Susie   Which meant that you couldn't come forward, you couldn't be playful with people.

Jo   I spent most of the time hiding in the toilet or smoking outside for something to do. I don't even smoke, but I did. I did feel the pity, I felt the pity, I don't know whether I expected it, so then I brought it on, you know this whole thing about what you think and you think it into happening, I think that is what I mean by have I brought it on myself, and ...

Susie   So did it mean that you didn't have any space to think after the reunion, I would really like to see X and go for a coffee with them, or I couldn't manage it that night because I was working and it was embarrassing for me. Was there no desire to pursue anybody?

Jo No, I felt totally, I felt like I was in the wrong world. I don't know where, if anywhere, I can belong.

Susie Um, that's really tough.

Jo I feel like I'm completely isolated from even my friends that I've known. I feel like they're miles ahead of me in everything, miles ahead of me in life, in the industry. I do feel like I'm being left behind, but I'm sick of feeling like that and I want to change it, but I don't know how to change it, which is why I'm here.

Susie Uh-huh.

Jo And I want to – I'm ready to change it, I am ready to rethink things, but I need some help doing it, because also I don't feel like I've always been like this. I feel like everything is getting on top of me, I know it is a cliché but it's – that's how I feel, and I'm slowly, slowly, removing myself from a world that I thought I belonged in and now I don't feel like I belong in it at all.

Susie I don't want to say platitudes, but you are in a world that is very difficult and a world in which a lot of people feel insecure and have infrequent work, but your difficulty is you don't feel you've got a purchase on that world now.

Jo I feel like I did, or I had the help that I did.

Susie So do you understand, when you felt you were part of it, what that was like and how or why it went wrong?

Jo Now it just feels like it was another life, or it was another me.

Susie	Uh-huh.
Jo	Or I've lost who I was.
Susie	Uh-huh.
Jo	And I've lost my love for life, or my …
Susie	Well, I think if you feel tipped out …
Jo	Yeah.
Susie	That is an accurate feeling which is really difficult.
Jo	Yeah, but I guess I want to do something about it.
Susie	Uh-huh.
Jo	And I want to learn, I want to feel those feelings again of, like, joy. I don't think I've felt joy.
Susie	From your perspective, Jo, what's the story you have in your head, because you've got a big story, which is: am I part of causing this? But what is the actuality of that, can you say? Can you tell me your last couple of roles and how you feed off the thing you love?
Jo	Oh God, I mean …
Susie	What they were? What they meant to you? What was the feeling in acting them and your engagement with whoever you were playing or with the director?
Jo	It's been so long, um, I feel like there's a part of me that's very scared to remember that because I don't have it, so I am scared to remember how good it was because my life is not that now.

I am trying to slow Jo down and attempting to move her away from two ideas that there is only depression or joy, horror or ecstasy. There are a lot of steps between being desperate and getting to neutral and being able to have ordinary pleasures in your accomplishments, with your friends, or your work, or nature.

When Jo left the stage, I have the sense that it was understandably hard for her to manage that disappointment. If she could, and if she now can, accept that disappointment she would in time be able to hook up with her energy and capacities rather than going to the grand dramas of joy or depression.

Susie   Yes, I am not suggesting this to make you delusional, I just want to understand when you say 'Did I cause part of this?', leaving aside chance, which is really big.

Jo   But in my – it's not really just about the – it's not just about acting, it's about my life in general.

Reading this back, I wonder whether I am pushing work difficulties while Jo is talking about personal relationships. In her initial session I got a sense about what went wrong with her ex and her humiliation about work friendships, so my focus, perhaps mistakenly, was to go where I sensed more grit on the one hand and I wanted to see what kind of elasticity of thought she had to come out of the 'fault' issue.

Susie   Yes, I understand, but it was your livelihood, and your form of expression, and your form of community.

Jo   Yeah, I guess it was, yeah, it was my community.

Susie   It was where you had a foothold or you felt you belonged.

Jo   Yeah. I guess right now, though, the only thing I can think about – you know people say it's vulgar to talk about money, well, you shouldn't talk about money.

Susie   Uh-huh.

Jo	And I feel like there is a reason people talk about money, it is because they don't have it, and it's very different if you've got money, you don't have to think about it. Suddenly when you are in a situation where you know you are having to pick up 5p pieces off the floor to buy yourself a banana, or to put towards getting something, you are thinking about money all the time, and the lack of it, and it rules your life, and I feel like I'm overwhelmed by it because I have always done the jobs that I have chosen, or jobs that have spoken to me, spoken to my heart, but now I feel like I don't know what my heart or gut is ever telling me because I feel overwhelmed by not having anywhere to live.
Susie	Uh-huh.
Jo	Um, and I don't feel like there's any space for what I loved, which was being part of a company, which was acting and investigating and exploring and being inside someone else's head, and now I'm just inside my own head all the time, and it's not a very nice place to be.
Susie	Uh-huh.
Jo	Ah, I want to get myself out of this rut, and there's only so long really I can be that friend who stays on everyone's sofa. It makes me feel pretty worthless if I'm honest, but I feel like I'm ready to, whereas before I felt very angry.
Susie	Uh-huh.
Jo	And I don't feel like that any more, I feel like something's got to shift.
Susie	Well, that's an interesting shift, isn't it, because it means, difficult as it is, that you are not fighting against the idea that you've got to find a way to look after yourself.

Jo	Yeah, I feel like I need to take responsibility for something.
Susie	And how you're going to do that in the short term and how you're going to figure out how to manage economically so you're not picking up 5p pieces.
Jo	Yeah, I know and that's the reality.
Susie	Uh-huh.
Jo	Or anything, 2p, 1p. Oh, yeah, I think it's difficult because I can't, I don't have the fall-back of my parents. I'm an only child, my mum is not in any stable situation herself to be able to help emotionally or practically.
Susie	Well, I think it's very hard to be orphaned emotionally and financially.
Jo	Yeah.
Susie	And not sure how to take which steps, and I think it would be helpful for you to be in therapy.
Jo	Yeah.
Susie	Yeah.
Jo	I think so.
Susie	Because it is a way to stop just going around the same ...
Jo	Yeah, I feel like I am in ...
Susie	A loop.
Jo	A loop that I can't get out of and I need to take that step for someone.
Susie	I think you've already taken the step by getting back in contact and accepting, I'm not where I want to be, but I'm really vulnerable and I need some real help with this.
Jo	Yeah.

Susie	And I know I have to do a lot of trying and thinking and challenging myself.
Jo	Yeah.
Susie	And I need somebody walking beside me to be helping me to think and do and work on that.
Jo	Yeah, that, because also I feel like it's got to be now because I feel like I'm turning into somebody that I never was or that …
Susie	Disappointment and loss and being evicted from work produce very difficult feelings.
	You have mentioned the word cynical a couple of times and I suppose you mean you are so hurt and you don't want to be cynical and bitter, you actually want to use your energy in a way that begins to calm you so that you've got some to take forward. So look, let me think about this, Jo.
Jo	OK.
Susie	I will get back to you.
Jo	Yeah.
Susie	Within the week.
Jo	With a suggestion of …
Susie	Yes, have a think. Just let it sit with me, I'll have a think and then I'll see if that place or that person …
Jo	Uh-huh.
Susie	Can find a way to see you. OK?
Jo	Yeah.
Susie	OK, alright.

Jo	Thank you.
Susie	OK.
Jo	Oh, just to check, um, do I pay for this session?
Susie	It's OK, don't you worry about that.
Jo	OK, thank you.
Susie	OK, alright, so give me a week.
Jo	Yeah sure, you've got my number right? Yeah, of course.
Susie	OK.

There is something warming about Jo having made contact again. I feel optimistic on her part. I know it is going to be a tough struggle whether or not she lands some theatre work soon. She is facing her defeats and the pain of her present, which has excluded her from the world of many of her peers. Like many actors, the characters she played helped her with a search for and an expression of her identity, and without the role to play she is forced into a confrontation with the confusing parts of herself.

There is a scandalous lack of provision for talking therapies within the NHS as posts are cut back and back. There is no parity for Mental Health services, despite governmental rhetoric, and voluntary services are stretched. The private therapy sector (within the psychoanalytic and Jungian wings) has always held to the principle of providing therapy at very low cost, which means that practitioners will often have a few hours a week set aside for a person like Jo.

Maureen

Maureen is seventy-five. She's been a carer for her mother, nursing her through Parkinson's. Recently she's been looking after her husband, who has dementia. She wears a dirndl skirt, a soft pink blouse and pink trainers. Her white hair, blue eyes and tiny, lined face is lively. She speaks softly, as though telling secrets. It is her fifth session.

Susie   Hello.

Maureen   Hello, it's Maureen Ellis.

Susie   Come on in.

Maureen   Thank you. Nice to see you again.

Susie   You too.

Maureen   Um, I, ah, I don't really know where to start today because I had a phone call this morning, from Guy. I don't know whether I told you about him, I met him when I went dancing, I started a dance class actually, I used to love dancing and I just go once a week, and I met this man Guy, who is very, very nice, and …

Susie   Uh-huh.

Maureen   He asked me out to dinner, and I don't know what to do, I don't know whether to go.

Susie   Do you know what you'd like to do?

Maureen   Well, part of me would love to go, I mean, I don't know whether I told you Susie, but, um, it's sort of embarrassing at my age, you know, but when I was dancing with him, I suddenly felt young again, you know, I felt just me, and it was wonderful. He's very tall, and I've had a knee replacement so I can do things I couldn't do before, and I sort of whizzed around and I did feel wonderful, like a person again, and I realised I haven't been a person, you know. When you care for somebody, you are a person, but you lose, or I felt I'd lost my identity.

Susie   Uh-huh.

Maureen   At certain points I did get my confidence again, when I was sort of taking care of him and we became a bit close at the beginning of his dementia, but then as it goes on …

[*Pauses and sighs*]

Sorry, sorry, it is getting so hard visiting him. I visited him on Sunday, and he was in a very bad place and he just makes these awful sounds now, and he's now been put in a dementia home, he's been taken away from this nice place near where I live, but been put in this place, and, um, it's horrid, it smells. And to see him, who was so alive.

Tom used to be so alive, so funny and big, and extraordinary, and so that's just, I'm sorry, I'm rambling a bit, I know, but this phone call has sort of put me in a bit of a position because, um, yes, to answer your question, I would love, I would love to go to dinner, um, but I am also scared to go to dinner, I haven't been out.

Susie   Uh-huh.

Maureen   You know, I do my evening class, but I haven't been actually out. When you are dancing, you are with a lot of people … he's got a wife with MS, who's in a home.

I have a feeling there's something there.

Susie   Uh-huh.

Maureen   Am I allowed to hope, to live, you know?

Susie   Your eyes are shining and you're smiling, and why shouldn't you have companionship and interest? You aren't walking down the aisle yet!

Could you explore going out for dinner?

Maureen   Actually you're right, you're right, I'm so aware of the judgements of, of, of Tom's friends and my daughter, who sort of goes on and on at me for not doing more and I wouldn't be able to tell her.

Susie   You don't need to tell anybody.

Maureen   I don't need to tell anybody, do I – just go, just go, and go home after.

Susie   You didn't ask for permission to take your course, your humanities course at Birkbeck.

Maureen   No, I didn't.

Susie   You didn't ask for permission to go dancing.

Maureen   That was me, wasn't it?

Susie   Yeah, and you found people to share the developing bits of your life.

Maureen   Yes, to meet people who have the same kind of guilt of, you know what I mean.

Susie   It's a very cruel situation, isn't it, because you lived your life ...

Maureen   With somebody, yeah.

Susie   With somebody, and then you lose them.

Maureen   And you do lose them because they're not, they're not there.

Susie   And you had this moment when you connected in a way that was post-children when he was first diagnosed that was so alive and then lost him again. You really lost him and you didn't even have that old relationship where you just knew each other. Understandably it's going to produce difficulties inside of you: confusion, maybe guilt, children, daughter banging on at you, your friends really not knowing what to say or what to do. Your dilemma is to hold all of them, but also to take up what you have been interested in, which is …

Maureen   Life.

Susie   Exactly, life, the reading, the dancing.

Maureen   Life. It helps me to hear you saying, Maureen, you did, you did your dancing, you did choose to study. I did, but you kind of forget yourself – do you know what I mean? – that it was you who did these things.

Susie   Yes, nobody told you to go and do a Masters at Birkbeck: you were the one who said I want to do this.

Maureen   Yeah, yeah.

Susie   You walked yourself in there.

Maureen   Yes, and I feel alive. My brain feels alive, and I think when you are caring for somebody with dementia you sort of, you spend so much time trying to understand them that your own brain feels as though it's getting smaller and smaller and smaller, and you're terrified that you might go the same way.

Susie   Yes.

Maureen   If you don't fight to break out …

About four months ago, I went to see Tom, who just makes these noises which are awful, and he was making them. I'd missed two weeks because I'd, well, I'd actually had my knee replacement.

Susie   Uh-huh.

Maureen   And I can't, I won't, do the sounds because they disturb me, but he suddenly said *I've been waiting for you for a very, very long time.*

Susie   Yes.

Maureen   And he spoke words, and it was like a light.

If a light is flickering, and then it's dead, you know that. But when he said that, I thought there is that light again, because I want to understand this dementia.

Does that mean that those words *I've been waiting for you for a very long time*, are underneath all the time? Do they understand? It was really upsetting.

Susie   I think what you are describing is flashes of presence.

Maureen   Um.

Susie   Emotional presence, but …

Maureen   It is like just a faulty light bulb.

Susie   I think emotionally it is like that for you, and that's all we can really work with. You find it hard to be sitting there with Tom, with the sounds, and no connection.

Maureen   Yeah.

Susie   Which is perhaps what your daughter keeps implying.

Maureen   Well, she thinks if I visited him more often he would remember me more, my face would be there, but I have been told by the staff, which does help me, that in fact, this sounds so ironic, but the fact is when I go he is sometimes more upset after because he does remember something, whereas if there is just a period of not me, there's this sort of, I don't know whether he goes onto this plateau where nothing is interfering with his, I don't know.

Susie   I think it is hard to know, and they've got much more experience.

The painful question is what you can manage.

Maureen   Yeah.

Susie   And it seems as though you can usually manage to go a couple of times a week.

Maureen   Yeah.

Susie   And yes, there was a respite for you while you were dealing with your own knee, the hard bit is seeing what can work for you.

Maureen   Yeah, I really need to study myself as much as I study a book.

Susie   Uh-huh.

Maureen   Or a thesis, or try to understand myself because I have found for ages you just, you've got such a routine treadmill, you just do things without thinking, and now it is helping me to come to you and realise what I'm thinking, and also to be able to talk.

Susie   Uh-huh.

Maureen   And to be heard actually. You hear what I say.

Susie   Uh-huh.

Maureen   I know that you do it all the time.

Susie   Uh-huh.

Maureen   I mean, that's your job, isn't it, but very rarely in life do people actually hear what you are saying.

Susie   Well, it's a dual thing: if you are heard, you can hear yourself.

Maureen   Absolutely, and have time to realise where you are. I've
                come now, I'm seventy-five. I come now and I am thinking
                these things, and you think back on all the years where
                maybe you haven't listened to people, haven't been heard.
                Why do you have to wait until you are very old, very, very
                old before you come to a realisation like this, or you've
                been through hell and high water.

Maureen is talking about a cultural phenomenon in which self-reflection or examination is not part of what we do, and the sadness she feels about having missed such personal contemplation. I'm also thinking of Maureen in her historical moment as mother, wife, daughter and carer in all these aspects of her life, and how she finally has a space to feel her own interests outside of the family.

Because she isn't attending to others on a day-to-day basis, she has the chance to hear her own desires and feeling. Her radar is not continually tuned to others.

Susie   Well, I am not sure the important thing is the why, the
                important thing is that you are.

Maureen   Yeah.

Susie   One of the things I was thinking about from our last
                conversation is, having looked after your mother, who got
                Parkinson's at a very early age, and you wanted to look
                after her, it wasn't …

Maureen   Um, I did, I did, I really loved her.

Susie   That it's, and then meeting Tom shortly after, it meant that
                your ways of being got tracked in a particular way.

Maureen   Yes, yes.

Susie   And I suppose what you have been able to do now is maybe pick up the things that you thought you wanted to do when you were younger that have stayed with you.

Maureen   Absolutely, and …

Susie   So it is the intellectual activity, but it is also finding a voice, finding a self, post-children.

Maureen   Yes, well, there's a very strange thing that happens when you get older, which is that you are very present with yourself as a child, your memories of your mother and your father, and feelings of what you first felt, like first love or, you sort of go back to that. You're very close to being a child, I don't know if I am saying this properly, but it's all very vivid, and I suppose when you grow up and you're coping, as you say, with things like looking after your mother, marriage and children, you're just getting on. Your whole life is care. And as you get older, I've only got what ten years, fifteen years at the most, I've got to make, I've got to make the most of them.

Susie   But is it possible that what you are saying is that, apart from the memories, what you've captured for yourself is this incredibly precious quality of your essence.

Maureen   Yeah, your essence, yes.

Susie   Very alive.

Maureen   Yes, um, sometimes if you go to a funeral of somebody …

Susie   Uh-huh.

Maureen   And they talk about somebody's whole life, and that person who you've lost, they sort of talk about the driving force that person had, and sometimes if it's a good service you think, oh, that was the essence of them, that was the root core of their being.

Susie Uh-huh.

Maureen Umm, and that's what you sort of realise as you get older – that was, that was who I was.

Susie Uh-huh.

Maureen I can remember a picture of when I was very small, and I was on a beach with my sister. I was very happy, and I just had my arms around her and I can now envisage that and get that wonderful feeling of no responsibility, just being one with the sun and the sea.

Susie Uh-huh.

Maureen I suppose ideally if Guy, instead of a meal, if we just went for a walk by the sea, that would be just brilliant.

Maybe if I go to dinner, I could suggest that next time.

Susie Uh-huh.

Maureen Do you know about recapturing something of the … of the past?

Susie You mean recapturing the innocence or the pleasure of the past but being in the present?

Maureen Yeah, just being one with the sea, yeah, do you know what I mean?

Susie You look at me like it is a little bit naughty, a little bit with a sort of …

Maureen I feel it is because …

Susie It's sort of excited naughty.

Maureen It is, it's a hoping and then feeling there's naughtiness. It's at the same time seeing my husband completely nothing, nowhere, uh, in a kind of, in a kind of hell, and I just find it, that's, that's the problem, that's the sort of, that image of where he is, um, and me going off, you know.

Susie Well, maybe that's why you have images of childhood.

Maureen Yes.

Susie Because it removes you from that anguish, whereas actually you are a woman of seventy-five.

Maureen Yeah.

Susie With a husband.

Maureen Yeah.

Susie Who's left, to all intents and purposes.

Maureen Um.

Susie So you are actually way past childhood and way past raising children together with him, and having a life.

Maureen Um.

Susie And you've got a lot of sorrow and loss. But you have also got something else coming in.

Maureen Um, I know, I see what you, where you are coming, you are saying grow up and stop being a child.

Susie I'm saying what's emanating from you is the excitement emerging from a seventy-five-year-old woman who has lived a life.

Maureen Yes, yes.

Susie Of course it has echoes of childhood, but it isn't a return or a replay.

Maureen Yes, yes, it isn't, it isn't.

Susie It isn't because it is …

Maureen What it is.

Susie It is what it is, and it's inflected or it's saturated with your history.

Maureen Yeah.

Susie And your present, which is not so easy, but it isn't only not easy, it has also got pleasures in it.

Maureen And he too, Guy, I mean, I know with his wife with MS, he probably has very similar feelings too, you know, and you need love in order to live, don't you?

Susie Uh-huh.

Maureen To go on, because there isn't anything else, is there?

Susie So you think you might allow yourself to?

Maureen Well, I tell you, when I was coming along today I was in a right old state, I think, but yeah talking to you I feel, I feel I owe it to myself.

Susie Uh-huh.

Maureen And also, I don't know whether you're saying this, but you're kind of encouraging me that because I have been through all those things I probably need to realise that, and, and I can probably help him, Guy. I mean, it's not just the little feeling in me of, I may, in my maturity, rather than it just being naughty, woah, woah, woah, but it's not wrong to use your experience in life to understand other people.

Susie Uh-huh.

Maureen And I've just been so cut off and remote with friends. Family needs have narrowed me, apart from my interest to care.

Susie   Well, you've had a very difficult situation to manage. You've had, from your account, a long and happy marriage.

Maureen Uh-huh.

Susie   And you've suffered a hell of a blow.

Maureen Well, it's sort of like a living death.

Susie   Yeah, and it's almost like an act of desertion.

Maureen Yes, you do feel … I felt he'd walked away, that's the difficulty. It's the coldness of walking away.

Susie   Umm.

Maureen They don't realise they look cold, but it's like walking down a road that you're not on but you've still been trying to help them down the road, but they don't see you and it goes on and on and on, and you get blamed sometimes for it.

Susie   Well, I suppose it's the terrible feeling of rejection when Tom went down that road and on top of that everybody having their opinions about what you should be doing.

Maureen Yeah.

Susie   And you getting a strong calling that you wanted to go dancing, and you like studying, and maybe you will go out for a walk on the beach or dinner with Guy.

Maureen I couldn't, I couldn't even have admitted that to myself unless I'd come here, and I tell you I really resisted coming to somebody to tell me what to do, I didn't realise, I mean, I remember when my mother died, somebody said you ought to go to the Samaritans or go to a counsellor to grieve, and this woman said you're not grieving for your mother, and I thought don't you tell me what to do. I felt quite angry, I felt I don't want to grieve, but I don't feel that now.

Susie   But you found your way here, and maybe you would have done it without finding your way here.

I think it is worth you remembering that the initiative to do things has come from you.

Maureen   Yes, yes.

Susie   So you might be able to take this initiative.

Maureen   Yeah.

Susie   So let's see, and I'll see you next week.

Maureen   Thank you, thank you very much.

Maureen's grace and her struggle have touched me considerably. She is less than a decade older than me, but because of the historical moment in which we both came of age, and, of course, our personal biographies and desires, she has had a very different life experience with children, husband and mother occupying her main energy. My generation developed a critique of the emotional and psychological costs of being brought up to see oneself as primarily a midwife to the activities and needs of others. There was a hard-won psychological struggle for many to dare to also answer to one's own personal needs. Maureen is coming to that now, and it is very moving to see her managing the pulls and guilt on the one hand and her desire to breathe a different air on the other. She is hardly abandoning the idea of doing emotional labour. She is seeing Guy as someone who can draw on her experience with being a carer who lost her mother and Tom, but she is also taking a delight – as am I – in her being able to pursue her intellectual, dancing and loving interests.

Afterword

The work of therapy is hidden and often invisible. People wonder what goes on in the room. Are therapists like the cabbie or hairdresser on to whom secrets are poured? Are we like the priest who hears confession? Does therapy create a dependent relationship? Is it all just psychobabble and self-justification? Is it a way of absolving oneself of guilt and responsibility?

As I hope I have shown, it is some of these things and none of them. In therapy, the opinions of the cabbie or hairdresser are absent. The quiet attention of the priest may be present, but it is only the starting point. Dependency may exist for a period of time. Strange-sounding phrases may be intermittently developed between the therapy couple. Guilt and responsibility get taken out of their rigid boxes, examined, and instead of being absolved, they may turn into other feelings or get reshaped.

Therapy, like any specialist work, can seem odd to an onlooker. It has been my aim as a psychotherapist, when outside the consulting room, to show what is so fascinating and potentially life-changing about the process and to apply the insights of therapy to the wider world.

I've wanted to show that therapy is a different way of talking and a different way of hearing. Therapy is as much a listening cure as it is a talking cure. The fact of being heard and of hearing one's words in a space in which they aren't necessarily interrupted or soothed but just hang, means they can reverberate. The individual (or the couple or the family) hears whether the words that have emerged are the right words. They are brought face to face with what lives inside them but is hard to say. Like words chosen for a poem, the clutter of daily language is eviscerated. The words might need to be refined, or they might shock the individual by being unexpected. Whatever they are, they carry a new weight.

Slips of the tongue, of course, can have significance, but beyond that, and in a more ordinary sense, one discovers, as one talks, the things that are difficult, the feelings that are rushed over, ignored or avoided. The words that resound, the silences, the ellipses, false starts, interruptions and hesitations which feature widely in the therapy, upend the conventions of ordinary conversation.

The patient, client, analysand (all unsatisfactory terms from my point of view, and thus I tend to use them interchangeably) enters the room. How she or he does it, whether she looks at the therapist or down at the floor or smiles or uses the same opening words, such as 'What a week!', are all artefacts of the therapeutic encounter, as is the therapist's quiet welcome. Delight, a hug as a hello, a soothing arm around a back, common in friendship, are absent. In its place the therapist conveys an intense interest in seeing the person. Her or his ears, heart and body are open to what will unfold in the session, a session marked by time boundaries and usually occurring in the same place.

Therapy, psychoanalysis, is a collaborative venture. Two people – analysand and analyst, patient or client and therapist – sit in a room together. It is a democratic process. The analysand initially drives the session because of what they bring, the way they set the conversation and the pace. As the relationship develops, the language that is created, the pauses, the reflections, the interjections of the therapist will be particular to each therapy relationship, quite the opposite of psychobabble. The rules of therapy are there to create the conditions for the work of therapy to occur. They do not impose a similar shape or feel on each therapeutic couple.

I am not the same therapist with the twelve people we have met in this book. Each one of them evokes differing aspects of me, uniquely draws on parts of my personality, taps on my heart strings with their own tune, or the tune I make inside of myself in relation to them. The way I feel about each of them is distinctive. What I offered was specific to them. Therapy is a bespoke craft, with each therapeutic pair, or group, creating novel circumstances to respond to.

We met Richard and Louise, a couple on the cusp of parenthood. They came because a distance had opened up in their relationship. Richard seemed to have disappeared into his work as a builder, and Louise, who had just taken a leave from her job as an events manager, felt abandoned and let down by Richard, a man she had adored until late in the pregnancy, when the fact of the impending baby became obvious. Their need was for some rather urgent reconnecting with each other, albeit on different terms from the enchanted romance that enabled them to be carefree until recently.

They are both engaging individuals, yet now disgruntled in their own bubbles. It's hard, except, for brief moments, to feel what they have between them. Instead I felt Louise's urgency and Richard's reluctance. They pulled on me in opposing directions. I pondered whether the poles they express in the sessions we listened in on are important features of their relationship in general or specific to late pregnancy and early parenting with its ensuing excitement and panic. I felt Louise's frustration and Richard's annoyance and fear. I felt the tug between patience and impatience. I wanted Louise to back off so that Richard could take up some space but I'm aware of a dynamic between them in which Richard will continue to retreat if Louise doesn't insist that he participate in their new adventure. He needs her to beckon him, and this is as true when their baby arrives as before.

Therapy is an emotional journey for the therapist, not just for her patients. Sometimes, as we saw, it's a high-wire act, as when John drops his unexpected bombshell. I'm on my toes, empathic and touched and trying to choreograph myself so that I don't puncture his dignity. Sometimes it calls for serenity and the simple wisdom of age, as with Helen, the young woman lawyer, who has been in therapy for twenty-four months. I remember the feelings she is so flummoxed by and feel the relief that I am no longer plagued with her questions. I want to convey that the questions and dilemmas she has are exciting, but I need to be mindful that the experience of longevity can sound patronising, which is not what I feel. I have been very moved by how her cancer diagnosis has shifted her into new territory not exclusively new but sharpening her dilemmas. With Harriet, a school secretary in her forties, I was asked to understand the most painful of losses and feelings of helplessness. I believe I was helping her with those feelings, but it will be a long haul and looking despair in the eye is not easy for either of us. With Jo, my compassion for her ineptitude mixes with exasperation as she unwittingly tests the boundaries of the therapeutic encounter whose conventions she does not yet know. And yes I was so pleased she was able to come back and consider getting help. With Douglas, his desperation calls me to want to act. With Charles I want to make him less suave and detached. With Natalie I want to hold my own frustration of not yet understanding what she's up to. With Maureen it's an easier call of straightforward empathy. With Amelia and Grace I live in both positions, as a mother and as a daughter.

When I take someone on for therapy, I notice a somewhat peculiar process occurring inside me as I take a walk or as I'm doing the washing or am on my own in a non-work situation. Unprompted, I hear their speech pattern in my ear. Or my body spontaneously imitates the way they move, hold their head, smile or grimace and settle themselves in the therapy room. So with Jo, I heard where she placed the emphasis in a sentence and I felt myself take on her winsome smile as though to find a way to make a space inside of me for her.

When you offer yourself as a therapist to someone you can't know how long the person will stay with you, but it could be for a considerable time. You are living their issues with them, and there is a way in which the intimacy that evolves requires me to open myself, my body, my ears, my eyes, my sense of smell, to fold them inside me. Their idioms impact on me from the outside and the inside. I'm not simply a technician of the mind's tributaries. My analysands get into my own bloodstreams of thought, feeling and movement.

Each person who comes to therapy needs the same thing – to be listened to, to be thought about and to be heard in a private space – as well as something distinctive and personal. A harassed woman may require a sounding board to check that she isn't too critical of her children, but it must be offered in such a way that she doesn't experience my responses as adding to her burden. Therapy needs to open some mental territory where she can think anew and afresh. A fifty-year-old man, sent to boarding school at seven, when his parents divorced, wants me as an approving appreciative mother figure. I feel it, but I know he can't have me as an ideal replacement. The grief he feels for his early disillusionment and loss will not be healed by a better version of Mum, however seductive and cosy that feels.

A twenty-four-year-old young woman wants me to be a more distant version of her very capable but, from her perspective, slightly invasive mother. I have to see my own self as someone who can respond to what she needs without undermining her mother. The couple who need to see that the very things that annoy them in each other are the parts of themselves they like to disavow, reminds me how a third person (the therapist) can tilt conversation to enable them to reknit their intimacy. The academically driven professor for whom feelings cause her difficulty has to be persuaded of the intellectual reasons for why emotions might be of value for her and why risking experiencing them with me will be useful. She likes to tussle and wants me to tussle back, and I do. It's the way to reach her, but it wouldn't suit many people. A man in an aggressive struggle with his stepson needs to know how his actions can have a positive outcome rather than a negative one. His reported conversations make me wretch inside, and the struggle to offer him an alternative puts me in a teacher situation.

Each individual who comes for help craves acceptance, even though they may be diffident or even tetchy. Knowing that craving provides me with the motivation to get underneath and behind the cruelties and difficulties that I am hearing about, some of which will be thrown at me unexpectedly. How can I be useful? What am I being asked to do? Who am I a proxy for? What will enable my patient to clear the space around them and consider something from a different perspective? How can I parse their feelings so that they increase their emotional repertoire rather than repeatedly play the same no longer productive song?

Such are the demands of the consulting room and what gets stirred up in the therapist.

The psychoanalytic session always has had a strong aesthetic for me. It is a practice like the work of painting or writing or composing or dancing or working on a scientific problem. It requires knowledge which constantly refreshes itself. It requires expertise, and it requires an ear to shape, feel and touch the heart of the issues so that they can be revisioned. At the same time there is a physical aesthetic, by which I mean the resonance and rhythm of a session, how noisy it is, the weight of the silences, the relationship between therapeutic dialogue and reflectiveness, the way the bodies in the room move forward and back into the shared space in response to intensity.

In Richard and Louise's session I felt an urgency to quiet the noise. I wanted to clear the jangle in my ears and slow the language into a different register. The jangle I experienced is an unthought-out signal that the contact between them needed reshaping.

There is a prosody in their dialogue, when each one talks without listening:

Richard   You're more interested in my mum than you are in me.

Louise   Well your mum's very helpful.

Richard   She used to hate Mum before, she couldn't stand Mum coming round.

Louise   I didn't hate your mum.

Or take my dialogue with Natalie in which reading this back I can see I copy her rhythm:

Natalie   I can't keep seeing Christopher, I can't keep doing that. I have to, I have to stop that …

Susie   And if you imagine stopping, if you imagine stopping seeing Christopher …

What constitutes the aesthetic of psychoanalytic therapy is harder to pin down. The aesthetic is not to do with harmony, because it can be decidedly unharmonious. I think it is probably to do with the struggle for truth. A provisional truth, to be sure, but an honesty to engage in a venture which presents itself like a mess of rubbish, with no coherence except for its capacity to make the individual feel help-less and hopeless. Through a process of clearing and examining, what needs repairing, what needs sorting, what needs protecting, what needs discarding, what needs nurturing, and in what order these things can be done, constitute an aesthetic. Marked by rhythm and timbre, by the idiom established in each analyst–analysand couple and by the pacing, something beautiful evolves at both a psychological and spiritual level.

Therapy is a deep practice. It searches for veracity. One truth can open to another which may shade what is first understood. The intricate constructions of the human mind shift during the course of therapy. Being a participant observer to the changing of internal structures and of the expansion of feelings is very satisfying. Seeing how defences are used, and how they can be worked around and in time dissolve, has a beauty which is perhaps akin to the mathematician or physicist's experience of finding an equation elegant.

I find the particulars of learning how an individual's internal world works fascinating. We are always learning. We all split parts of experience off, like Natalie and Harriet and Charles. We all forget. We all protect ourselves against certain ideas and feelings. We do this because, if we remembered and felt everything, there wouldn't be much psychic space for the present. While psychoanalysts theorise our ways of understanding the mind and the body, the work of brain scientists and neuropsychologists is dovetailing with what we discover in the consulting room. As we understand the compelling nature of the pull to repeat what may ill serve us, so the neuroscientists are attempting to plot the ways in which the mind prunes and shapes experience through repeated actions and beliefs. All three disciplines confirm the evidence that the essence of the human is the consequence of our long learning outside the womb. We don't arrive knowing how to walk and talk and think and feel. We arrive with the capacity to do so and we apprehend specifically how in the context of the relationships which receive us. Those relationships, embedded in time and place and economic circumstances, then structure our mind, our feelings, our brains, our desires, our behaviours and the way we are embodied.

Therapy takes so very long because the structures of mind we develop in infancy, childhood and adolescence are quasi-material structures. They are who we are and, although the human mind and brain have great plasticity, desired change can be very difficult. Psychoanalytic therapy, with its emphasis on looking behind our defence structures to the beliefs and feelings that can appear dangerous or unknown, involves the therapist serving as an external anchor (hence the caricature of being over-dependent on the analyst) while the work of deconstructing and reconstructing follows. In therapy you don't just learn a new language to add to your repertoire: you relinquish unhelpful parts of the mother tongue and weave them together with the knowledge of a new grammar. The curiosity a therapist has towards the analysand's structures designate us as anthropologists of the mind. Each individual mind embodies complex understandings of social relationships – the interplay between self – what is allowed and what is sequestered and what to do with what isn't allowed. To know an individual is to know some of their time in history, in place, in class, gender, caste, race and the society and family constellation they have emerged from. An individual is the outcome of her or his engagement with others from birth (and, some would argue, the womb) onwards.

As we unlearn and remake, so we impact on those we are close with. We all know this in a matter-of-fact way: a bully can intimidate. An easy, confident person can make us feel included and capable. A puffed-up show-off can make us feel competitive. Our minds are both resilient and flexible. We can explain Stockholm Syndrome or the affection built up for an abuser by the mind's capacity to make accommodations to need. In therapy, however, the way one mind has an impact on another becomes part of the subject of the therapy. This makes for an intensity and truth-seeking which forms part of the aesthetic.

So what difference does therapy make? Why should someone come? Does everyone need to come?

Many live with painful family secrets which can erupt at Christmas or when the family gets together. Many live with unease or are beset by symptoms that intensify. Many feel an emptiness or a confusion about why they can't activate their desires, or why they sabotage the things they imagine they want. For others, their relationships unravel and devastate them and they don't know why. Richard, Louise, Harriet, Helen, Jo, John, Amelia, Natalie and Charles were in difficulty. That's why they came. For Maureen and Douglas, talking with family or friends had not reached the places that could help them sufficiently. John tells movingly of the aliveness that he now feels, as though before he was walking through life not living it. He's not alive because he's fallen for me. He's alive because he's fallen for himself. Yes, love can look like the catalyst but a more important catalyst was my being deeply interested in him. He found a way to open himself up. He began to see himself as being of value: to himself and to me. The negative self-image he carried didn't just dissolve. He'd had to work hard not to slot the attention he's been receiving into a set of categories that nullified it; 'she's just doing her job' (true but nevertheless what makes for the healing). Or, 'if I show her it is affecting me, she'll have power over me', and he had to risk being vulnerable to me in order to change himself inside.

Love, of course, does do that – temporarily. It allows us to see ourselves differently because we are loved and do love, but if love itself isn't sufficient for change, because the patterns that hurt can be stimulated in a new relationship, then therapy can be of profound help.

With Harriet, therapy is about addressing a present wound that has activated a previous loss that ruptured everything she knew about life. She didn't just lose her father; she lost her mother too, because despite her mother being with her, she was divorced from her own home and community. The bereft mother conveyed a resigned attitude about getting on with life which left a depressive hole in Harriet, which she coped with well enough until the failures of the IVF and her own flight from her partner. Harriet's present loss is allowing her to face the earlier loss from which she cut off as she turned herself into the nice girl who could try to fit in. Her earlier depressive disposition will clear. It will become reconstituted as a loss, and that will restore something that she's been missing without knowing it.

Listening to Helen, we hear her desire to understand the meaning of life. It's a big question which will be made up of many small answers. When I say that we are working to rearrange Helen's internal furniture, I mean that the structures of her psyche need to be reorganised so that she can discover what she wants and join it up with an emerging Helen inside of herself. Such changes won't be easily integrated in the first instance. They involve reconsidering her job, her boyfriend, her relationship to her parents, her health and her interests as she struggles to expand herself from the inside out and not through her accomplishments. Doing so – as we have seen with the cancer scare – is giving her a time of questioning and the desire for a life of meaning. It won't be without sadness, sorrow or disappointment, for those are parts of life, but she will have embodied Freud's famous dictum, to move from hysteria to ordinary human unhappiness.

Helen has similarities with several young women that I have seen in my practice over the last twenty years or so. They share a sense of having fulfilled their dreams by getting good jobs, nice enough housing, boyfriends, looking great, being very social, and living a metropolitan life. The heartbreak for me is that this is a generation of women who, while they have grown up with the promise that the world is their oyster, have often not had the emotional support to implement it psychologically. Their teachers and parents have told them they can go far and have held open the doors and applauded them. So, what do I mean when I say they haven't had the emotional support? The ability to jump through hoops and overcome obstacles has been expected while conflicts and fears they feel about 'advancing' are not really addressed. As feminism in the noughties moved out of political discourse it was replaced by a bizarre assumption that women (and indeed men) can have it all if they tick the right boxes. The importance of conversations about what it means to be breaking new ground has been replaced by an over-optimistic and individualistically focused 'you can do it' philosophy where success is measured by position, money, advancement, looks and an externally positive attitude.

Paradoxically, the very processes and conversations that enabled women in the 1970s to dare to take up new possibilities, the support from contemporaries and the understanding that such daring was both hard and exhilarating, was either not known about by the next generation of parents or was deemed unnecessary since they themselves hadn't gone through it and the world had appeared to open up.

The bequeathing of ambition – often by mothers like Helen's, who had not pursued her own – was loving, but it may have been an ambition which denied the fear or the struggles there might be at a psychological level. Thus the complexity of what the young women were engaging with was often hijacked by them finding the next mountain to climb, rather than acknowledging the difficulties they would or could encounter inside their heads and hearts. The internal voices or conflicts would be silenced rather than have room to breathe and in time dissipate, and this has added to Helen's plaintive words *What is the point?* and *I suppose I feel lonely quite a lot of the time*. In this sense I feel excited that Helen is asking questions about existence and recognising her inner loneliness. It is a good prognosis for her to put her inner life and her outward achievements together.

D. W. Winnicott, a psychoanalyst and paediatrician, understood very deeply the problem of internal alienation. He called this dilemma the False Self. He saw the True Self as an undeveloped part that had not been nourished into life. He proposed that when the main parent, usually the mother, is unable to see and respond to the desire of the child, the True Self goes underground. Resourcefully, the child then finds those aspects that the mother can respond to. This makes the mother feel good in what she is then able to give and the child feels good that he or she has mother's approval and attention. As this pattern of pleasing continues, the True Self fails to come alive and be real for the individual and she lives by the compensations the False Self can garner.

The False Self has many attributes and can serve the person well up to a point. Then a chasm between the search for the next challenge and a nourishing life can open up. Helen got to that point, which is why she sought therapy. In her therapy we have been working to understand the False Self organisation as she tentatively invites the dormant True Self to peek above the parapet so that she can get to know her. In time the False Self (which is better called an adapted self) will join up with the True Self (which is better called a more authentic Helen). She will be enriched and feel she has herself with herself.

Helen has grown up at a time of enormous social change in Britain. Most of the social democratic values that shaped the world after the Second World War have been slowly dismantled. Consumerism, the notion of the individual as a brand and the prevalence of digital life and social media have changed the terms of growing up, especially for young people who have economic resources. The focus on individualism and making it, doing it, being it, selling it, is new. Life can turn into a performance. I've encountered several young women who come in saying their lives are devoid of meaning and purpose. They say that everything is going well on the surface but they feel lost and empty. They have rituals they subscribe to, either around eating/not eating, going to the gym, meditating, socialising lubricated by alcohol and cocaine, which they see as crucial. They are digital natives who live with medium-level anxiety a great deal of the time. If we put together the social changes with the psychological difficulties these intensify, we should take seriously the empty feelings many are expressing as an indicator of social and personal malaise.

Jo presented us with a different dilemma. She came because her friend had told her to. She's lost. Her acting different roles gave her ways to imagine and play a life but not enough grounding to find truths for herself. Her bubbly, pleasing persona is shielding a more desperate stance which therapy will be able to address so that she can stop bobbing around and find what she needs to know about herself in future. Her courage in returning and not running away from herself and her very real difficulties is hopeful. She's been dealt a difficult hand and she is trying not to flee from it. Richard and Louise have had quite some readjusting to do. Becoming parents is an opportunity for each of them to create a present they both can live in with their boy rather than repeat their history and the history of their parents. And this is a salient fact of therapy, that history can be in the past rather than unknowingly casting its pall over the present. The past acknowledged allows for a richer, layered and less fearful present. Amelia and Grace are shifting their relationship as Grace is coming into young adulthood. It's fraught and tricky and both the role of the parent and the role of being a teenager have dramatically transformed since Amelia was young. Fortunately, their good humour is allowing them to find a new way of being together and a new way of talking. Douglas, forced to examine how his private life is interrupting his professional competence as a judge, finds a route into compassion for himself. Charles's nonchalance has been threatened and he faces some challenging encounters with his wife, his partners and his son. Natalie has to tolerate being confused until she can link up the bits of herself that have been compartmentalised. With Maureen, we see her struggling with the end of one kind of life and the risk of opening up to another in which her personal desires are more apparent. Accompanying each of these characters is a joy.

But I haven't answered the question of whether therapy is for everyone. For me the answer is no. Therapy is one kind of vector into that wonderful adventure, an examined life. It is an intimate and delicate route but makes little sense unless one is in psychological trouble. Yes, we can all benefit from becoming emotionally literate, and social programmes which help expectant parents, educators, doctors, nurses and so on expand their own emotional knowledge are effective ways to enable us to know ourselves, to connect well with others and be alright in our own skin.

For others, art, literature, bonding through sport, political or spiritual activity, satisfying enough work and so on will provide meaning. But it is an arduous struggle in a time of political cruelty which wreaks extreme economic and social division, while despoiling our environment and creating divisions inside us.

Many live lives of quiet desperation, as Henry David Thoreau told us in *Walden*. Therapy cannot answer these ills on its own. Psychoanalytic ways of thinking have much to bring to public policy and the political conversation, whether about the family, child development, bonding, body image, emotional collapse, unwanted teenage pregnancy, repeat offenders, gangs, violent or abusive relationships, attachment difficulties, compulsive eating (or not eating), smoking and cutting, alienation, war, fears of immigrants and turning groups of people into 'others' and so on. In a time of fake facts and the drive to over-simplification, complexity of analysis is imperative.

Like other disciplines such as sociology, economics and social psychology, psychoanalytic thinking should have a place at public policy tables as its insights speak to the mismatch between people's inner and outer experience – the gap between what they say and what they feel, which no other discipline addresses. Psychoanalysis studies people in the process of change, illuminating unexpected reasons and motivations, which, if understood, could lead policymakers to different emphases as they try to effect wanted social change. In this sense psychoanalytic thinking, as a technocratic discipline, has something to bring to the table alongside other analytic methods, not in the way of behavioral economics with its notion of nudge. Psychoanalytic prompts are in a sense anti-directive and thus expansive. Psychoanalysis can never supplant other forms of research, but it can enrich them.

Symptoms of distress in our society are exacerbated by changes in global culture and the development of rampant consumerism, which is itself a pointer to the horrors of ordinary needs for connection and contribution not met. We are invited to participate in society by taking up identity markers such as brands and viewing ourselves as a brand. A sense of belonging is fostered by purchasing, but its falsity fails to satisfy. So, too, are fundamentalist modes of thought, whether they are xenophobias, nationalisms, racisms or gender hatreds. In fundamentalist modes of thought, only a narrow band of feelings can be tolerated and solutions to injustices are expressed through adherence to political, sectarian or religious party lines which have a hard time with complexity. They abhor internal dissent while thriving on external disagreement. What consumerism and fundamentalism both highlight is the human desperation to belong. This is not pathological: the desperation to belong is what makes us human. When we belong, we can feel safe being separate. We need separated attachments. If we don't, the expression we find for it when it goes awry can be deadly and this is part of what besets global culture today, the promise yet often impossibility of belonging.

So therapy for everyone? I say no. But therapeutic ideas to enter social discourse? I say yes. We don't and can't fully know ourselves. That is a conceit to protect us from feeling vulnerable and helpless. Much of what we do and how we go about it is unconscious. Therapeutic ideas can't make us fully conscious but they can make us less arrogant and more humble in a generous manner about what it means to be human and to live.

Like literature, psychoanalysis reveals the commonality of human experience by drilling into the particularities of the individual. The way an individual imagines and projects, the way the individual reads and misreads situations, speaks to us in our own private struggles. A highly personal and specific story unfolds to reveal common human themes.

As we unpick what drives each of their behaviours, we come across the human search for secure attachment and recognition and the ways in which that search becomes derailed. We know about this. It's why we cry at the cinema when the lovers come together. We understand that longing. We feel that longing. We may crave that belonging. The specific tells the general. And so it is with psychotherapy. Each story tells us about the individual or the couple while it tells us about ourselves. We want to know about others' struggles because we want to know more deeply about ourselves and the project of being human.

Appendix: The making of the programmes

Writing about clinical work and what actually occurs in the therapy is hampered by the confidentiality of the therapy relationship. It makes transcripts of actual sessions nigh impossible. I have tried to solve the problem of how to invite the reader into the feel of what occurs by using actors to give a sense of the taste and flavour of an encounter.

My aim in making the programmes out of which this book came was to get as near to the experience of the consulting room as I could. In previous books, *Fat is a Feminist Issue*, *Understanding Women*, *What Do Women Want?*, *Bittersweet* and *Bodies*, I wrote about what I was discovering about longings, conflicts and confusions and used vignettes to describe and theorise the process of therapy and the theory that Luise Eichenbaum and I were developing.

In *The Impossibility of Sex* I wrote a set of imaginary cases told from the point of view of a fictionalised version of myself. I wanted to convey the craft of the working therapist breathing, sweating, being challenged, while thinking and feeling her patient's dilemmas. Kevin Dawson, the producer, had read it, pitched it to the BBC and they offered us a series of fifteen-minute programmes for

Radio 4 about the process of therapy. I knew I didn't want to script something; that would not show how therapy actually goes. I had recently done a couple of mini-therapy-type sessions with actors in a Wallace Shawn play directed by Ian Rickson. They and a series of sessions done earlier with Kate Bland for Cast Iron Radio and for an initiative by Jordan McKenzie for The Gay Men's Choir, had taken the therapy out of the consulting room without abandoning the conventions of the therapeutic session. I knew Ian's genius with actors (we had occasionally worked together in the rehearsal room over the years when he was doing a new production), and I hoped that he would be able to choose and prepare actors to take part in a series in which they become characters who are in therapy with me.

The play scripts that have emerged convey the feel of the consulting room. These encounters were not in any way scripted. They are the embodiment of what the characters expressed: characters who come to the therapy in search of understanding and relief from their anguish, confusions and problems.

The three of us met for what was to be a first for all of us. Kevin had little knowledge of therapy but knew how to produce, Ian could choose actors who were strong on improvisation and I had to stay as true to my craft as I could with the wrinkle that I would pretend to know the people coming to talk with me in my consulting room.

People who have listened to the radio programmes have imagined that I carefully drew out a list of specifications for the characters. Not so. That wouldn't have felt real to me. People are always more surprising and layered than a description can be, and the unfolding of that is one of the great joys for therapists in the consulting room. I suggested very little to Kevin and Ian in our meetings beyond the barest of outlines. I said I wanted to see a couple whose difficulties might be linked to patterns in their parents' relationships. I suggested a woman in her forties who might have emigrated early on in her life. A sixty-year-old trade unionist whose second marriage had broken down and who was feeling desperate. A young woman in her late twenties or early thirties who appeared to have everything but felt nothing. A first session with someone whose work life had not panned out.

From these rudiments, chosen for no particular reason except to give the range of a therapist's working day (although less various than a working week's practice), Kevin and Ian worked up a back-story. I knew that pretty much whatever they came up with would be alright because fiction, while less dense than the facts of an ordinary life, can nevertheless show so much more about a life than a simple narration in non-fiction. Thus I wasn't worried about authenticity. I knew it would or could be.

With barely three agreed sentences on each character, Ian worked closely with the actors to embody and grow these personae. I was reluctant to use actors whose voices were familiar on radio, as I didn't want to draw the listeners' attention away from the therapy process. When Liz White, playing Louise, walked in to do the couples session, I had a faint sense of recognition. Later, I realised it was she who had been giving birth in *Call the Midwife* the night before on TV. Peter Wight, playing John, is an actor with tremendous presence who I'd seen on stage several times but in roles with enough variety that I couldn't quite place him, and that was a guide. Noma Dumezweni, playing Harriet, had not yet been cast in *Harry Potter*, and Noo Kirby, playing Helen, was not yet Princess Margaret in *The Crown*. Nat Martello White, playing Richard, and Sinead Matthews, playing Jo, were highly accomplished on the stage too, as are Simon Shepherd, playing Charles, and Vinette Robinson, playing Natalie, thus known to a smaller not radio audience. Perhaps our only radio exception is Anna Calder-Marshall, whose voice many will know. All were and are superb actors, but not so starry that the audience would be focused on their other roles or personalities.

The set-up to record was clean and simple. Perhaps not so from the sound engineer, Gareth Isles's, point of view. I wore an unobtrusive wireless lapel mike, as did my 'patient'; we recorded in my consulting room, with me sitting in the same chair as I habitually do; and two rooms away Gareth created an extensive recording studio. Kevin wanted to ensure the sound would be good enough to pick up nuances of breath, sighs, tears or whatever was to emerge.

Before the session started, when the actor was being miked up and getting a final prep from Ian at a local Caffè Nero, Kevin and I would talk about who was coming to see me that hour. I tried to familiarise myself with their backstory from a paragraph that Ian had given me.

The doorbell rings, and the person comes up the stairs. I greet and welcome them. There they find two large beige leather chairs, a brown leather sofa with blue cushions, a blue Caucasian rug by a large window overlooking a garden, and many, many books.

They sit on the sofa and talk, or not, as would be the case in any session, and then at about the twenty- or twenty-five-minute level, the length of half a session, I bring it to an end. We both walk out of the consulting room and into the ersatz studio, where Ian, Kevin and Gareth are sitting with cans on their heads.

We debrief, the actor goes off and we do the next session.

Later on, having listened to the recording and worked out how to edit down to the prerequisite fifteen-minute broadcast in a way that retains the integrity of the session, including the pauses, we meet to do finer cuts and voice-over. Therapy is not entertainment, like a mini-radio play or serial whose conventions we have absorbed. It can crackle with intensity, but it can be laboured or sound incoherent. We wanted to keep the feel of all of that and I believe we did.

Therapy has its own dramas. We make different kinds of patterns and linkages in the therapy room. Sometimes there will be a startling interpretation which will thrill a radio audience by its unexpected capacity to change the direction of how someone feels and perceives things. Equally, listening in to therapy would turn out to be quite unusual radio. The individual is looking for the words she or he wants to say, the patterns that need to be made or the emotions that need to be undammed. It's not neat, and it doesn't follow a straight-forward narrative. In any given session insight might happen, but sometimes the job of the therapist is to sit and hear and absorb and make oneself available for moments of connection. It can be anti-drama. The focus when cutting the programmes was to be faithful enough to the process of therapy.

I didn't set out in this series to show what happens when misun-derstandings occur, but of course they are inevitable. Therapy will sometimes engender misunderstanding, and when this occurs, the therapist tries to address it.

We use the therapy relationship a bit like a laboratory. When something goes amiss between therapist and client or the words or intentions of either are misinterpreted, that becomes part of the work of therapy. We call this process an enactment, and in the sessions we see several examples of this, most notably in Jo's first session. The question then became how to keep enough of the 'enactment' in the programme so the listener might understand how the therapist deals with it.

From rough cuts we went into a studio to do a series of explana-tory voice-overs. Kevin wanted these outside of the therapy room and in a studio in order to create a different soundscape. These were conducted in a conversational way and spliced in. Ian's genius was to prep the actors, but in doing so, he was of course having to think about how to direct me, without appearing to. I am not an actor. In talking about it subsequently he said he did so by ramping up the number of tricky things the improvisations would throw at me so that I was in a heightened state. In this way he created mini-psychological conundrums for me to respond to.

Despite the artifice, these mini-sessions convey the flavour and feel of the therapy room. Together the three of us and the individual actors had found a way to mimic the aesthetic arc that would end up on radio.

Acknowledgements

My thanks:

To Sinead Matthews, Noo Kirby, Noma Dumezweni, Peter Wight, Liz White, Nat Martello White, Anna Calder-Marshall, Vinette Robinson and Simon Shepherd, the superb actors.

To Ian Rickson and Kevin Dawson for such an enjoyable working relationship. To Gareth Isles for sound engineering that really works.

To Gudrun Wiborg, Luise Eichenbaum, Brett Kahr, Caroline Pick, Sally Berry, Jane Haberlin, Gillian Slovo, Kamila Shamsie, Sian Putnam and Barbara Nettleton.

And to Penny Daniel and Andrew Franklin, my lovely and very capable editor and publisher.